ELISABETH WYNHAUSEN was born in the Netherlands and grew up in Australia. She is a respected journalist who has worked for *The Bulletin*, *The National Times* and *The Age*, both in Sydney and New York. At present she is a senior writer for *The Australian*. Her first book was a memoir, *Manly Girls*.

DIRT CHEAP

Life at the wrong end of the job market

ELISABETH WYNHAUSEN

Pan Macmillan Australia

Names of individuals and organisations
have been changed throughout.

First published 2005 in Macmillan by Pan Macmillan Australia Pty Limited
St Martins Tower, 31 Market Street, Sydney

Copyright © Elisabeth Wynhausen 2005

All rights reserved. No part of this book may be reproduced or transmitted in
any form or by any means, electronic, mechanical, including photocopying,
recording or by any information storage and retrieval system, without prior
permission in writing from the publisher.

National Library of Australia
Cataloguing-in-Publication data:

Wynhausen, Elisabeth.
Dirt Cheap: life at the wrong end of the job market

ISBN 1 40503644 3.

1. Wynhausen, Elisabeth. 2. Journalists - Australia - Biography. 3. Labor - Australia. 4. Wages - Australia. 5. Hours of labor - Australia. I. Title.

070.92

Papers used by Pan Macmillan Australia Pty Ltd are natural, recyclable
products made from wood grown in sustainable forests. The manufacturing
processes conform to the environmental regulations of the country of origin.

Set in 11.5 pt Janson Text by Midland Typesetters
Printed in Australia by McPherson's Printing Group

For my brother Jules and his carers

Contents

Acknowledgements	ix
Prologue	1
1 The Club	13
2 The Factory	41
3 The Office	81
4 The Hotels	107
5 The Store	147
6 The Homes	187
Epilogue	231
Endnotes	238

Acknowledgements

I may never have finished this book without the unstinting support of my friends Sandra Levy, Aviva Ziegler, Susie Carleton, Helen Scott, Hilary Linstead, Ed Campion, Tom Dusevic, Bruce Sims, Natalie O'Brien, George Megalogenis and Kyrsty Macdonald.

I am indebted to Michael Stutchbury, the editor of *The Australian*, and Chris Mitchell, the editor in chief, who gave me leave and leeway.

I received generous assistance from Michael Lye, Iain Campbell, Jeremy Vermeesch, John Buchanan, Annie Owens, Andrew Casey, Jane Farrell, Craig Thompson, Brett Holmes, Rod Young, Jenny Fallon and Campbell Reid.

Particular thanks are due to my ever-patient and helpful editors and former editors at Pan Macmillan – Alex Craig, Karen Penning, Bernadette Foley and Robyn Flemming – and my agent, Fiona Inglis of Curtis Brown.

Most importantly, I owe a great debt of gratitude to the many people I worked with – without them there would be no book.

PROLOGUE

AT THE AGE OF 55, I made a spur-of-the-moment decision to take nine months' leave from my job as a journalist with *The Australian* newspaper. I wanted to see if I could get by as a minimum-wage worker and live to tell the tale.

I'd been inspired by the book *Nickel and Dimed: On (Not) Getting By in America*, Barbara Ehrenreich's account of her odyssey as a minimum-wage worker in the United States. Instead of tracking down people earning poverty-level wages, Ehrenreich had tried it for herself, finding a job as a waitress in a Florida diner for US$2.43 an hour plus tips, and seeing if she could live on it. Her book vividly depicted life on wages that were so low, 'trailer trash' was a 'demographic category to aspire to'.

The thought that someone should try it in Australia persuaded me to ask my editors for leave without pay. My mother said I was mad. My friends tried to talk me out of it. But I never had a doubt about the preposterous decision I had made: I would take time off the newspaper to work as a cleaner or kitchen hand, a sort of self-funded sabbatical on the breadline.

I found the idea exhilarating, as if I were embarking on an adventure that would give my life new purpose and meaning. The prospect of stepping out of my usual life may have resonated more strongly because my parents had done so twice over. They fled Holland in 1942, and left by choice in 1951, settling as far from Europe as they could, like so many other Jews who survived the Holocaust. I didn't know much about the war, *their* war, growing up. But even as a small child just transplanted to Sydney, I was aware that my parents, my father in particular, dreaded going door-to-door asking for work in halting English. I would remember that when I went door-to-door asking for work in a country town, as if I were perversely compelled to endure some small part of what my parents once endured. We had been in Australia less than a year when my father, who had found work with a meat company, fell while unloading a side of beef. He fractured disks in his spine and was laid up for months. With less-than-fortuitous timing, he had bought a milk run just before the accident. My mother delivered

PROLOGUE

the milk before seven in the morning, hosed out the truck, saw my brother and me off to kindergarten, then drove to the edge of civilisation to sell fabrics door-to-door, lugging the heavy suitcases of materials on and off the truck.

This ordeal made a profound impression on me. I had no way of helping my adored mother (though I tried as best I could, scurrying underfoot as she carried the suitcases back into the house), but after I picked up an arts degree in about twice the usual time and got my start writing about show business for a Sunday tabloid, I gravitated towards subjects that involved a generic settling-of-accounts.

The view of society you get from newspapers is as indistinct as the view of the street from the highest floor of a city building, that being the rarefied top-down perspective journalism habitually adopts. The most influential journalists are typically players more interested in shaping events than chronicling them: although they may quote the cab driver they meet on the way from the airport to Parliament House, or from Parliament House to lunch at Ottoman, their real contacts are important people who also understand the game. I'm more intent on vivifying the flash of colour and the blur of movement down below. I prefer to be in the thick of it, a perspective better suited to telling the other side of the story, like the glorified tale of the economy, furiously hyped as 'the miracle economy' even as it widened the gulf between winners and losers in a nation that once led the world in social mobility. When the new millennium dawned, executive salaries in Australia grew 26 per cent in a single year. The declared taxable incomes of the top 5 per cent of taxpayers had risen by 31.7 per cent between 1995 and 2001, about five times the rate of increase for people on average earnings.[1] The wage-fixing system that had protected the wages and conditions of workers was gradually unravelled. Trade unions came under assault. The government promoted individual bargaining while limiting trade union access to workers. But the workers didn't benefit from the deregulation of the workplace. Nothing had grown faster than the number of jobs that offered no sick pay, no holiday pay, and no job security beyond the next shift. Nearly nine out of ten jobs created in ten years of almost uninterrupted growth paid less than $26,000 a year; half paid less than $15,000.[2]

Some details emerged before the Australian Industrial Relations Commission (AIRC) from year to year when the Australian Council of Trade Unions (ACTU) bolstered its case for an increase for those still on award wages with witness statements from low-wage workers. One woman told of not earning enough to have her television set fixed for months after it broke down. The Australian Chamber of Commerce and Industry countered that a television set was an *entertainment device*, not a household object.[3] This was the kind of big picture that provoked me to zoom in on the small one: what is it like to scrape by on minimum wages of $11-something, now $12-something, an hour, as millions of Australians and their families do every day?

PROLOGUE

I was under no illusion that what I was embarking on would replicate the situation of people with families to support. Unlike them, I wouldn't suffer unduly if I lost a casual job or couldn't find one. I had money in the bank – $20,000 I put aside in case all else failed. I didn't pay rent. There was no mortgage anchoring me to my salary. Trying to live on what I earned was the starting point of the project. What drew me on was the hope of animating the experiences of a class of people who had remained invisible even as their numbers swelled.

Since I was starting off with nine months' leave, including accumulated holidays, I decided I could fit in half-a-dozen jobs, staying in each for two to four weeks, which would give me time to rough out a chapter before I looked for work again. I made up some rules, most of which I would break. I would apply for any unskilled jobs I saw advertised and take the first one I was offered. I believed I would find work, if only because I'm good at talking my way into things. The real question, as my friends frequently reminded me, was whether I would keep a job for long enough to have something to write about.

While willing to undertake whatever work I was offered, I decided in advance that I wasn't prepared to put up with the accommodation available to low-paid itinerant workers who needed lodgings on a week-by-week basis. Whatever else I was doing, I would have to go home from the job to make notes, which tended to rule out shared rooms in backpacker hostels. I would need a room of my own, but I drew the line at a room in the sort of hotel where you shared a bathroom down the hall with cadaverous old men. I rather carelessly assumed that I would tailor my budget to what I was forced to spend on accommodation. I based my assumptions on full-time earnings. But I soon made the transition that typifies the new, deregulated workplace, going from a permanent job to a casual one, and from permanent work to shiftwork, not knowing from one week to the next if I would earn enough to live on, a common fate for the casuals in the fastest-growing sector of the workforce.[4] But people were counted as employed if they worked more than one hour a week, which kept official unemployment figures much lower than the real figures even as the legions unable to find full-time work drove up the numbers on unemployment and disability benefits.[5]

I borrowed the address of a colleague who lived in Auburn, an industrial suburb in Sydney's west, and made up a cover story that left out 30 or so years of journalism. I claimed I had re-entered the workforce after many years as a housewife and had since worked part-time as a cleaner and function waiter. It was easier to concoct the first half of the résumé. I'd worked in shops as a student, and only had to fudge the timing, stretching jobs I'd done in the holidays into years of life experience. I threw in references from friends willing to say I'd cleaned their houses or carried trays at their functions. They knew I was honest and reliable, after all – or had been before I started lying to employers about my age and experience. If the official line on the subject was any guide, I shouldn't have found it necessary to lower my age in order to get a job. Intent on minimising the numbers claiming the full pension, the government maintained the fiction that the first wave of baby boomers were succumbing to the lure of the golf course rather than being thrown on the scrap heap.

'We have to recognise that the cult of early retirement ... should be changed,' Prime Minister John Howard said in November 2002 while addressing the annual convention of the Financial Planning Association. By then, 46 per cent of people aged between 55 and 64 had *no* paid work, and older workers reported applying for hundreds of jobs without so much as a nibble from an employer,[6] but the prime minister was calling for a relaxation of anti-discrimination laws to allow employers to advertise for older workers. Under the guise of its so-called national strategy on ageing, his government was starting to pressure over-fifties on unemployment benefits to look for work. Who can say what would have happened if I'd admitted how old I was – I always whipped off ten years, hoping that no one would ask for my driver's licence.

I was like an amateur criminal at first, shaking with nerves if I had to wait for the interview long past the appointed hour. It was standard to be kept waiting fifteen to twenty minutes. The less people pay you, I found, the less they look on your time as something you still cherish. I would sit there consulting my watch, worrying about being identified as a journalist, and clutching my fraudulent résumé and references in my clammy hand. The idea I'd be identified came to seem vain by the time I'd been hired a few times, using my name. No interviewer looked at it twice. None of them ever suggested I was anything but the person I claimed to be. In case there was something about me that didn't seem to fit my story, I had taken the precaution of saying that I had lived in New York and London while married. The only interviewer who mentioned it was in the hotel business and may have counted it useful for dealing with guests. I boasted of no other professional qualifications. I usually wrote that I had graduated from high school, but I varied the story now and then by throwing in a year or two at university. If boredom set in because I had been filling in application forms all day, I would admit to a university degree, or nominate 'reading' and 'writing' as my hobbies. It made no difference. I was applying for manual work but had failed to grasp its nature. I couldn't help thinking I'd get a job because I was smart and interesting. But what employers wanted to know was if I could get to work by six in the morning and had a functioning vehicle. Now and then they warmed up if I cracked a joke. 'I wouldn't have a job if you paid me,' said a bloke who ran a packing shed in the country. 'I was thinking more the other way round,' I said, and he told me to come back in a week.

Since I only had to find jobs to last me a month at most, I was prepared to do whatever work presented itself – the measure recommended by the theorists on over $150,000 a year fulminating from their easy chairs about 'people for whom working has become more trouble than it's worth'.[7] Let *them* go door-to-door cap in hand. I tried it several times, not sure how else to find a job in a hurry, and even got some jobs out of it. But unlike my fellow employees, I could quit any time I liked.

The other difference between us was that they could do the jobs and I couldn't. They may have dropped out of high school while I went on with my schooling, but whether we were mopping floors in a nursing home or packing boxes in a factory, it was the job we were doing that defined us.

I would go home after work each day to record what I could of the day's events. If I had started at six in the morning, I had a swim to wake up, then spent an hour or two at the computer, before one working day blurred into the next. On my last day on the job, I came out to my fellow workers whom I felt I owed an explanation. The confession generally fell flat. None asked me about my project. I assured them I was concealing their identities and that was that. I could conceal *their* identities, but I was soon to have trouble with mine. I had relinquished my position in life only to find I sorely missed its benefits. It was excruciating walking into an office to tell someone staring at me as if I'd just tracked dogshit over the floorboards that I was looking for work and willing to do anything. Is it any wonder that job-seekers routinely subjected to such slights grow too discouraged to look for work? I felt humiliated by it, although I was a confident person playing a part. But the confidence that helped me to find employment could be something of a hindrance on the job. However cautious I was at first, I usually ended up arguing with supervisors my co-workers tolerated because they needed the job.

I had expected to find myself in my element among them. The year before I started this book I visited a small town to interview workers whose factory had closed down, spending most of my time with a family whose class attitudes were so ingrained they didn't trust most members of the town's middle class. I got in under the wire. The wife said she found me easy to talk to. Much the same thing happened when I interviewed striking coalminers or unemployed steelworkers, hard-hats who drove utes with hunting lights and rifle racks. In general their interests and ideas could not have been more different from my own. We shared some political sympathies, nothing more. But there was an unspoken connection – or so I liked to think, remembering other trips. I had driven to Blayney, in the central west of New South Wales, to cover the closing of the local abattoir. I talked with everyone from the mayor to the men propping up the bar of a draughty old pub, but what stuck in my mind was the interview with an unemployed slaughterman in his fifties, in the crowded little sitting room of his home. He had a friend with him, a fellow meatworker and union official, who perched on a sofa that was too small for him. I would highlight the poignancy of their situation by writing that the men looked out of place amidst the lace curtains and cupboards filled with fussy ornaments. But the interview went on until late. I was in no hurry and I stayed to hear them out. I felt very much at ease around blokes like that. I liked to think they accepted me for myself rather than as a person with privileged access to the media. This illusion would be shattered soon after I began life as a low-wage worker.

Chapter 1

THE CLUB

I TIPTOED ALONG THE hallway to the reception area of the Club, feeling that I had strayed into the wrong half of some *Upstairs Downstairs* fantasy. I was there not to apply for membership, but for a job. The luminous hall, with its green-damask walls and huge bowls of rhododendrons, looked like a setting for *Masterpiece Theatre*, the distillation of theme-park English class. The pictures were better, though. A voice pierced the clubby stillness. 'Do you remember Margaret Olley?' a woman with silver hair said to her companion. The Olley hung off to the right. There was a Fred Williams to the left. I didn't dare to get up from the sofa where I'd taken a seat to inspect them, lest someone thought I was casing the joint. I assumed that sitting still and smiling with forced cheerfulness would make me seem dim and compliant. And I felt compliant, not like my normal self at all. I was obsessed with the thought that I would be identified. I didn't know that I was about to enter a world in which even people I had met would give no sign of recognition when I served them.

The Club was hiring kitchen hands, according to the display ad in a local paper. The advertisement said the 'outstanding' candidates 'must be honest, courteous, reliable and punctual', all of which presented less of a problem in the short term than the fact that kitchen hands are usually males half my age. I had called and left a message, but didn't expect a call back.

I had left my newspaper that week, but I had been combing through the classifieds for the past month. I'd had two interviews to show for it. Not sure how long it would take me to find a job, or even whether I'd find anything, I had decided to stay on in my flat in Sydney for the time being. I had bought a cheap one-bedroom flat on the cliffs at Bondi when I was in my thirties and owned it outright. I was lucky to have purchased it long before the smart set moved into the area, driving up real estate prices, but it now presented me with a logistical problem. I couldn't just charge myself a market rent and subtract it from my earnings – rents in the area far outstripped the incomes of families relying on minimum wages. Instead, I planned to find a job first, then look for accommodation close by. I should have guessed that I was more likely to find a job in an area where I couldn't afford to live on low wages.[1]

Jill, the fast-talking manager, turned up after I had been waiting for half an hour and promptly offered me a position in the cafeteria. She asked why I had applied. I said I wanted a permanent job, and that was it – I got it. It seemed absurdly easy. I had called about a temporary job at a chicken factory on the outskirts of metropolitan Sydney, in a blighted area where one or two tiny grocery stores had automatically activated bullet-proof screens, but more than 500 people had already applied. I hadn't been able to get temporary work packing frozen chooks at five o'clock in the morning, in a neighbourhood where bullets flew about. And yet, at a time when most new jobs were casual, I was being offered a full-time, permanent position in a club known for its association with old money. Part of the explanation revolved around $2.55 an hour, the difference between the $15.50 an hour the factory paid and the $12.95 an hour I'd earn at the Club. Without weekend penalty rates, the yearly salary was a modest $25,589.20. It was less than Frank Lowy, the shopping centre magnate, earned in a day, but, according to the 2001 Census, it was more than half of all employed women and 40 per cent of the total workforce earned.

I could readily supplement my salary, according to Jill, who said that since I would have the same two days off each week, I could go on doing any other jobs I might have, like domestic cleaning.

I was shown over the place by the assistant manager, a fresh-complexioned man with the trace of an accent, who seemed to imply that the job could involve some culture shock. Dieter was new to the place himself. As we wandered past glass cabinets filled with trophies and photographs of long-dead members holding antediluvian tennis racquets and croquet mallets, Dieter explained what the members expected of the 'help'. They thought of the Club as their home and at home they had servants. 'But they're very nice,' he said quickly. 'If you mention that your dog is sick, the next week they will ask you how the dog is.' I must pretend to have a dog, I thought. In the event I pretended to have children and grandchildren, but I could never remember how many.

When I started work the following week, Tina, my new supervisor, asked me if I had children. I invented a grown daughter and two grandchildren. I imagined I needed some explanation of my résumé, which, like the Nullabor, had long stretches of nothing between the little outcrops. I later realised that I had misplaced one of them when Tina, who was about to be a grandmother herself, asked me about my grandchildren again. I dare say she didn't notice. Endlessly distracted by the demands of her job, Tina flitted from one task to another. She had worked for the Club for seven years but seemed insecure about her position there. During the stocktaking at the end of the month, I saw her with a pair of scales and a look of pale, puffy seriousness, weighing a single banana.

On my first day, Tina marched me along a basement tunnel lined with laundry baskets and showed me where to find a uniform. It was navy, with white cuffs and collar. I had last worn a uniform at school; getting out of my clothes and into uniform felt like I was relinquishing part of my identity. Tina then led the way upstairs through the special staff door and along a hallway to a large, light, airy room set with chairs and tables.

This was the Buffet, the glorified cafeteria where I was to work. I was immediately out of my depth. Luckily, Lesley, the woman appointed to train me, was unflappable. Short and pretty, with her fair hair pulled back into a ponytail, Lesley explained everything with grave patience, showing me how to make the iced coffee the bluebloods consumed by the bucketload and how to fix their sandwiches. These were served on plates decorated with the Club crest – the same crest that had caught my eye when I saw the job advertisement. We had to make sure that the crest could be seen on one side of the sandwich, put a bit of tomato and parsley on the other side, swathe the lot in plastic wrap and put the plates into a glass cabinet so that they all faced the same way. This was clear, even to me, but when Tina bustled past, she took one look and decided to repeat the lesson. 'The crest faces the member,' she said urgently.

I had never before had to worry about the fine points of display and as I watched Lesley cutting sandwiches into perfect triangles – 'points', as I had just learned they were called – I said that I had really applied to be a kitchen hand. 'This is better,' she said firmly, suggesting that this work would keep my mind more active than being stuck out the back washing up for hours. The important thing was not to panic, she said – the fundamental rule in a business where the customers surge in like the tide at certain times of the day.

By lunchtime there were so many members and guests lined up waiting to be served that they seemed to be multiplying by a process of parthenogenesis, like amoebas. I hadn't seen so much privilege on the hoof since 1967, the year I took off from university to teach English at Frensham, a girls' boarding school on the other side of the Great Dividing Range. I would never forget the first day of term when I was bailed up by a pack of Frensham mothers who addressed me in accents so refined I felt I was being flayed with dipthongs. Thirty-something years had passed, but I kept imagining I could hear them all over again. Spotted in quick, dazed glimpses from our side of the display cabinets, the members all looked alike. They had silver-grey hair and wore polo shirts. It would have been hard to tell them apart, except that certain women wore madras-checked bermuda shorts and over-enunciated each word, as if talking to someone simple. It didn't help me much. I would take an order for a toasted sandwich and then stare wildly, too frightened to say I didn't have the faintest idea if the battleaxe who had demanded the beef and asparagus no butter (and no 'please' or 'thank you') was the one in the navy polo shirt with the yellow

Club logo or the one in the yellow shirt with the green logo.

Growing more flustered by the moment, I forgot to make a sandwich, then forgot it was my order. While Tina apologised to the member at the top of her voice – and her voice could have stripped varnish from timber – Lesley whispered, 'Don't panic, just fix it,' her hands flying over the wooden board as she made up the sandwich. I was convinced that I had just blown my career as a food and beverage attendant – and a sensational opportunity to observe downstairs life amongst the remnants of a class system already out of date when I was a girl.

I soon gleaned tidbits about the Club's exclusiveness from my fellow employees, who included groundsmen and sports pros, waitresses, receptionists, office clerks and chefs. The only time anyone had seen a black man in the Club, management came and warned them beforehand that a certain prince 'from Swahili-land or something' was expected. People with money couldn't just join, a waitress told me with a perverse sort of pride. While other clubs struggled to build up their membership lists, the Club put would-be members through a decade-long initiation test. They had to find a proposer and a seconder who had been members for ten years, and another four referees who had been members at least half as long, and then, all being well, they were placed on a ten-year waiting list. If they were still alive and kicking when the ten years had passed, they had a membership fee of $10,000 to pay, though by that time, of course, it was bound to be more.

Nevertheless, changes in the social composition of the Club reflected changes in the composition of society, since financial deregulation had assisted the rise of the working rich. The landed gentry who once formed the backbone of the Club had been replaced by surgeons, solicitors and self-made businessmen. Newish money was edging out the oldish. 'There are people that are members now my grandmother wouldn't have had in the house,' a man I know told me. This wasn't always evident from the wrong side of the counter. I had been to parties with the eastern suburbs set who were first-generation members (the bright, shiny businesspeople my friend's grandmother wouldn't have had in the house). I noticed that I felt a little gauche around them. That particular form of self-doubt had afflicted me as a girl, but not often since. My life was arranged to avoid it. Like most of my friends, I had gravitated towards a professional world in which people were judged by what they did, not by where they came from. But success in that déclassé milieu was leached of meaning in the context of the Club. Beneath their coating of assurance, some first-generation members may have felt they had got in by the skin of their teeth. But from my side of the counter, I saw clumps of incredibly privileged people, locked into the social certainties of a layer of society concerned only with its own preservation. They spoke in accents as brittle as glass, the younger wives carefully copying the hauteur of the older ones who had been around when they didn't let people in trade through the front entrance.

Slippery as the concept of class could be even on its most hallowed grounds, the Club tried to buttress it by constant recourse to rules and traditions. Only the previous summer, the eleven members of the committee had chosen to have a trial period before changing the rule that said gentlemen must wear long socks on the golf course. For the three months of the trial the men wore short socks if they liked – and then the committee decided to keep the long socks rule, after all. It wasn't practical, but practicality ran a poor second to the reiteration of the class divisions on which the Club continued to trade. Doing so in the new millennium presented a challenge which the committee dealt with by maintaining the barriers between members and staff. There were staff entrances, staff toilets, even staff plates. The Club gave employees sandwiches and soup for lunch, along with leftovers from the Buffet. But this was no simple matter of slinging yesterday's unsold salads and cakes on to the trolley with the staff sandwiches it was our job to make. The leftovers were still sitting on members' plates, but food for the staff had to be on staff plates. Tina would instruct one of the Buffet employees to transfer the food from one set of untouched plates swathed in plastic to another. Then the second set was wrapped in plastic, the only thing as expendable as our time. The sets of plates didn't differ much. One lot had a darker crest. Staff plates had once been members' plates, I guessed. Then they were relegated Downstairs for all time.

This reverence for tradition seemed to suit the older

members. They didn't much like change – not even change in the composition of the people in uniform. 'There's a lot of you new here,' said one old gentleman irritably, inspecting me over the counter as he had just inspected the roast pork and the soup of the day. I never heard members say much about the food, however. And if they did have complaints about it, these paled into insignificance next to the crescendo of complaints about the service the instant there was a lunchtime stampede of matrons in tennis dresses – surprisingly *short* tennis dresses – and crusty old geezers in long socks. It was hard to say if life had prepared the older crowd for the concept of self-service. But one thing was clear: they didn't like to wait. It impinged on their sense of entitlement. 'We all hate this system,' one said in a fit of passion, bumping her tray along for emphasis as she handed me her membership card to run through the computer.

The British children's books one read in the 1950s were suffused with sustaining myths about class which suggested that well-bred people had a kind of nobility about them which not only shone through when they were dressed in rags, but showed in their dealings with underlings. The residue must have buried itself in my brain, because I was startled by the members' lack of decorum – as if the elderly WASPs behaving like spoiled children were letting down their team. While we were earning $12.95 an hour, less than they paid for a roast with veg and a pot of tea, they were convinced they were being ripped off. One member, with the same last name and the same preserved-inaspic appearance as a second-rate British actress from years gone by, would order up big to impress her friends, and then make a scene about paying for it *after* they had scoffed the lot.

Of course, there were also members who were unfailingly polite, the one sign of distinction readily categorised by the staff. One member, a lively, dark-haired man who was often at the Club for breakfast, once turned up triumphantly waving the *Daily Telegraph*. It was easy to find that opinionated leftwing rag the *Herald*, he said. But he always had trouble laying his hands on the *Telegraph*, which gave him just what he wanted from a newpaper – sport and the crossword. If a newspaper *had* to have opinions, they should be on the opinion page, not the front page. He wasn't very smart, he said comfortably, but he had opinions of his own. He hadn't breathed a word, though, about the cost of the food or the speed of the service, the subjects on which we were routinely addressed by other members.

Some seemed to feel they not only owned the Club, but us with it, giving them *droite de seigneur* over our cramped quarters, which had a microscopic kitchen galley to minimise slips and spills as the chef glided from benchtop to stove. In the middle of the day, seven or eight employees bustled about the confined kitchen and the passageways behind the counters. Those in the galley could keep an eye on the Buffet by bending down and peering through the space between the benchtop and the cupboards in case anyone was waiting to be served. But just as we could look out of the kitchen, members could look in – and seeing common people working for a living got right up their wrinkled noses, apparently. One committee member who had campaigned to get something done about it finally succeeded: builders came in early one morning, before we were at work, and covered up the space between the benchtop and the cupboards with stainless steel panels that walled in the kitchen.

I had landed in the workplace equivalent of the land that time forgot, a strange, backwards-looking social laboratory of fast-vanishing attitudes, ideas and customs, some of them apparent relics of the days when staff who were paid a pittance lived on the premises, like family retainers. Others in the hospitality industry are under constant pressure to perform. But the Buffet had seven people doing the work of three or four, so that members wouldn't have to wait a second longer than necessary when they wandered in for a cuppa after a stiff morning of bridge or tennis.

While trying to absorb the fundamentals, I was confronted with a wealth of finicky detail about everything from the correct presentation of the condiments to the dimensions of the plastic tray and the paper doily required if a member ordered five sandwiches ('fingers' not 'points') for herself and her bridge partners. I was more accustomed to people who ate everything in sight, with or without a doily.

'I'm not in the mood for too much filling,' a grey-haired woman with an aquiline nose said one afternoon, sighing deeply at the exhausting necessity of having to choose a sandwich at all. 'What about smoked salmon?' I said. I hadn't been there long. My feet were killing me. 'What about curried egg . . .?' I paused, seeking inspiration. Lesley appeared at my elbow, whispering to me to let the woman decide for herself. She had silenced me more than once when I had forgotten my place and had chatted with a member across the counter. When I commented that I couldn't get used to members ordering me around like a servant, she said sternly, 'I don't think about it, I just do my work.' She was one of ten children and grew up in an area of Lancashire so poor that all the neighbours were on welfare. Lesley didn't believe in it. Her father had taught them to be self-reliant. 'I like to do things for myself,' she said one day as we walked out of the Club at lunchtime to get some air. It was typical of her to wait until she was off the premises to talk about her personal life. Her strong sense of propriety was of a piece with her sturdy independence and her pride in doing a thing well, as if something deep inside her forced her to be vigilant, to make sure she never sank back into the world that once surrounded her.

I was touched by Lesley's resolve to show me the right way to do things. On my first day at work, I had trashed a pair of rubber gloves in a vain attempt to extract the metal containers from the bain marie. I then watched Lesley lift them out with graceful, economical movements. 'They call this work unskilled, but there's a hundred skills to it,' I said, impressed. Lesley liked that. 'You could do a certificate in it,' she said, showing me once more how to perform the task. While eager to share all she knew, she worried that I would think she was putting herself above me, and said more than once that she wasn't giving me orders.

A number of my co-workers had taken me in hand. Janet, a big woman whose warmth and humour were hidden behind a fearsome scowl, was from England, but was a shade less resigned to the class differences that gave the Club its reason for being. Something more immediate was on her mind, however. Six months pregnant and intent on the life growing inside her, she spoke about it with a ferocious determination to do right by her baby. Though she hadn't been well, and walked heavily, as if her legs hurt, Janet was quick to help if I hesitated over something. On hearing that I hadn't used an espresso machine since about the time they were invented, she decided to teach me. When I attempted to copy her, I scalded the milk. 'Lash it,' she said cheerfully. She was from Liverpool, and used expressions I'd never heard before. Lash it? 'You mean toss it?' 'My words exactly,' she said.

I emptied out the metal jug, refilled it and promptly scalded the milk again. You can tell from the smell, even if you lack the kitchen gene. Before she went through it again, no-nonsense Janet asked me if I was sure I didn't mind her telling me what to do. It was a reminder – if any were needed – that the sum total of her knowledge and life experience was discounted to about $13 an hour plus penalties where applicable. (Penalty rates still applied on weekends in clubs in New South Wales, a benefit that was disappearing from other enterprise agreements.) It didn't provide much of a cushion to fall back on, and Janet dragged herself to work even if she felt rotten: she needed the money for baby things. Her husband was a labourer. Soon they'd be paying rent and all their household expenses out of his earnings.

Others at the Club had second jobs just to get by. Flame-haired, 36-year-old Estelle worked as a barmaid one or two nights a week. After a day's work at the Buffet, she would stand behind a hotel bar on the other side of town for five hours, to pay off debts that had mounted up when she was earning more. She was renting a flat rather than paying off a mortgage, so all those hours on her feet were for nothing, she said.

I was working with people who paid such a large chunk of their income on housing that a few struggled to cover basics like home repairs and school excursions. Housing close to the big cities is slipping out of reach of people on low incomes. According to the Australian Housing and Urban Research Institute at the Royal Melbourne Institute of Technology (RMIT), buying or renting housing close to the major cities subjects most low-income families to 'housing stress' by forcing them to spend more than 30 per cent of their income on the roof over their heads.[2]

Some choose instead to move out of the city. One of my co-workers, a trainee still finishing her studies in hospitality, lived with her parents 80 kilometres from Sydney and spent five hours a day on public transport. Another, Sally, a lively, pug-faced woman of about 40, travelled to work from a far-flung suburb on the other side of the metropolitan area. She had re-entered the housing market after some years overseas and said she couldn't afford to live any closer to the job. But she wouldn't stay put forever, she told me one day when the two of us were at smoko, out in the grim little loading dock where employees competed for space with trucks parked to make deliveries. I had asked if she rented her house. I was keeping score. Four of our eight co-workers owned a stake in a property somewhere. But Sally said she didn't want to tie herself down. She was involved with someone – a man she met when they were both changing trains one morning on the way to work – but said that in a year or two she was thinking of heading north to start a new life. She was still searching for something. But Sally was not typical of my new co-workers. What had struck me was the stability of their lives. Many had worked at the Club for three years or more, managing to keep their cars on the road, a roof over their heads, even a smile on their faces first thing in the morning, despite the grinding hardships of life on minimum wages.

I hadn't put my wages to the test. The Club was in a mansion-speckled part of Sydney where the only person with cheap housing had laid claim to a bus shelter that even buses seemed to avoid. Rather than moving to another part of the city, I stayed on in my flat. I went home from work early the first week, because I was on trial. But after a medical examination that included a urine test for what the doctor insisted was blood sugar, rather than drug-use,[3] I was given regular hours. My shift included Saturdays and Sundays, which added $114.92 to my gross salary. I was now pocketing $485.52 a week, considerably more than the vast majority of women in the workforce. Since I didn't need to pay rent, and was still struggling to adjust to the demands of the job, I staved off the attempt to live on my earnings, but I lived simply. I rose at seven and went swimming. The sun was still shining when I caught sight of the beach again on my way home. I would have liked to join the crowds of corn-rowed Brazilians practising capoeira and the Russians in their lipstick-pink tracksuits but my feet hurt. Rather than walking along the beach, I went home and showered before sitting down at the computer. I cut back on spending, saw very little of my friends and stopped going to my favourite Bondi café for breakfast.

My shift started at half-past eight or nine. I would march through the Buffet and the big dining room next to it into a cosy green reading room furnished with bound sets of books in glass cases. The day's newspapers were there, laid out on a coffee table. Stealing a furtive look at the front page of *The Australian*, I would grab a white apron from the stash hidden in a cupboard so that the chefs wouldn't find it, and tie it carefully. Tina had seen me wandering around one day with my apron tied so that it sagged and told me to fix it, suggesting that I'd be in deep shit if someone important saw it. 'They'll say something. It won't be pleasant,' she said. I hadn't been reprimanded about my uniform since I was a pupil at Manly Girls High and wore white socks instead of the regulation fawn. Lots of girls did. It made the headmistress apoplectic. And I was having sock trouble again. Our uniform included black shoes and black stockings. Because my feet hurt so much after standing all day, I put black socks on over the stockings. Between the uniform and the clumpy lace-ups, the white apron, the tea towel dangling from the apron, and the bits and bobs I had shoved into the apron's front pocket, the carefully turned-down socks were hardly more than a grace-note. It wasn't as if I'd given in to temptation and wrapped a brightly coloured do-rag around my head to complete the resemblance to one of those dumpy Russian street-sweepers shown brandishing their brooms in old posters – evidence of their status as Soviet workers. I was wrong about the socks, though. 'If Jill sees them, you'll have to take them off,' Tina said.

Jill enforced the rules that were the bedrock on which the institution was founded. There were rules about every facet of Club life, from the table ornaments to be used at Christmas-time to the way to spread the dining-room tablecloths. The central fold had to run north–south rather than east–west, or maybe it was the other way around. Jill was reputed to be able to spot at a glance if the cloths had been spread the right way – if not, she whipped them off and did it over. And not just the tablecloths but the tables had to be set out with mathematical precision, as I learned late one afternoon when I heedlessly straightened some. The quiet of the afternoon had been shattered by the arrival of a dozen or so white-clad women bowlers who had rearranged some of the tables to have afternoon tea together. 'Large pot of tea three pots of water,' one bellowed as if I might well be hard of hearing, looking not at me, but at the macadamia nut slices.

'They're a bit spoiled,' I whispered to Paula, a heavy woman with a big stomach and a bold laugh who had worked in the Buffet for six years, nearly as long as Tina.

'You've no idea,' Paula said, speaking under her breath. 'Yes madam, no madam, yes sir, no sir, have a good day, sir . . .'

When the dear old things left at last, I cleared the tables and numbly wiped them down, wondering if I was starting to adapt to the deadening routines. My reverie was interrupted by Paula, who liked to stir things up but was now looking sombre and fussing over the arrangement of the Buffet's nine tables. They couldn't just be scattered around the room, she said. They had to be lined up in three sets of three. That's what Jill said. 'If she feels so strongly about it, let her fix them herself,' I replied, and a shadow of fear passed over Paula's round face.

If you were rostered on until the Buffet closed for the evening, and another pink-cheeked Panzer division turned up for tea five minutes before closing, it would be well past six by the time you finished wrapping up the leftover pastries (tossing them out if you dared – 'housecleaning' we called it) and totting up the registers. When I saw Jill, I said something about it. 'You're signed out at six, but you end up staying longer.' Jill was unimpressed. 'There's lots of slow times when you stand twiddling your thumbs,' she snapped. But standing twiddling your thumbs was still standing. I had leaned on the counter one afternoon, to give my poor chafed feet a bit of a rest, but one of my colleagues hastily told me not to – leaning wasn't allowed, however busy it had been at lunchtime, however quiet it was now. One had to stand poised as if ready for action, even if there was nothing going on.

Confronted with regulations calculated to remind them of their insignificance, some of my co-workers reacted to the chance to show their authority like starving people flung a few scraps, fighting each other for the crumbs. I was given a hint of this early on by a middle-aged receptionist I had asked where I could find the time-sheets. She answered me with a long silence and a hard stare, as if bolstering her own position by letting me know where each of us stood in the caste system below-stairs. 'Don't worry about her – she's a bitch,' Paula shouted across the kitchen.

I was usually there, loading and unloading the big dishwasher, using unfamiliar muscles to stretch or bend to put the scalding just-washed china back on the shelves. I ached to say I wasn't doing too badly for someone more accustomed to office work. By the end of the third day when I had spent hours dishwashing, I just ached.

But in some respects, employees at the Club were better treated than is usual in the industry. Staff meals may be subsidised but are seldom free, even in clubland, but *the* Club gave employees free soup and sandwiches for lunch and proper hot meals on Sundays. It was as quaint a custom as I would come across during my time as a low-wage worker. In accepting the first job I was offered, I had unwittingly joined an establishment intent on preserving old-world standards. It worked both ways. Promotion was elusive – some said non-existent – and employees generally seemed to be stuck in the jobs they started in, like servants indelibly marked as members of the lower orders.

If it came to that, the free meals were a feature of attitudes so paternalistic that working at the Club was a bit like being at school in the early 1960s. There were rules about the requisite state of your nails – 'Fingernails should be clean and well manicured' – and rules about what you were allowed to watch on television. That one was on the noticeboard in the airless staffroom, along with the daily bulletins about the school reunions and wedding receptions that brought the Club a piece of its income. The notice said that staff could only watch the news in the morning and that the TV set had to be switched off between midday and 1.30 pm unless you had special permission from the manager or general manager. The little I had seen of the general manager made it hard to imagine asking him if I could watch *Days of Our Lives*. I passed him once as he marched through our domain, blow-dried and as blandly handsome as a Ken doll. I had expected a slight nod, if only to acknowledge me as a fellow member of the species, but the general manager looked at me with all the interest he might have shown a cane-bottomed bistro chair.

The official tone of the relations between the Club and its workers was conveyed by the vice president's words of welcome in the brochures handed out to new employees. 'You are now part of a large and happy family of members and staff.' First you had to be initiated, however. Constantly dogged by the fear that I would be found out, I panicked when Tina told me to go to the office, forgetting my position long enough to conclude I was about to be presented with a confidentiality clause. I decided to make a run for it rather than sign anything. There was no document, though. The Club hadn't anticipated a breach of confidence by a sandwich-hand known only by her first name.

Forced to wear a badge with 'Liz' on it, I still flinched each time a member addressed me by name. It made me feel like some object on which they had a claim. I was tempted to throw the badge away, but the rules said that badges had to be worn at all times. If you were a middle-aged woman in uniform members needed something to remember you by. They called me 'Liz' and I called them 'Sir' or 'Madam', just like the rulebook said. I didn't mind that part. The sirs and madams I gave the death stare were the ones who barked orders at me as if we were on parade.

There were two places to get away from them. One was the constricted-seeming staffroom where I wiped down the tables. The other was the loading dock, where employees were permitted to smoke. It was a dump: a small patch of asphalt a few metres wide, with kitchen trolleys lined up along one dank brick wall and empty milk crates stacked against the other. The crates did extra duty as seats. Inside the Club were hundreds of chairs, but all the loading dock had in the way of proper seating was a splintery old garden bench and two broken-down chairs. The whole effect was so stagily unkempt that the view of the treetops in the distance made me feel I had been locked up in some parallel universe.

Of course, you could always sit there on your broken chair, thinking of something a world away. One day a wiry Brazilian woman who worked as a room attendant in another part of the Club told me about the wonders of Brazil. In the Amazon there were pink dolphins. The Indians believed they were a god, she said dreamily, as if that far-off place had seized her in its spell. Then she stubbed out her cigarette, got to her feet and went back to work. I blinked and saw the loading dock again. It still resembled a prison yard. When I said so to one of the groundsmen, he decided to warn me that I couldn't trust all our fellow employees. 'If this was a war,' he said, 'the whole place would be full of spies and collaborators.' There were a few small kegs near his feet, part of the junk that was generally left lying around. But with Rafe in full swing, the kegs suddenly resembled footlights. There were dobbers everywhere, he said, insisting that eavesdroppers listened in on conversations from behind a blackened window nearby. Then he marched over to rap on the wall. 'The walls have ears,' he whispered in his raspy smoker's voice. It was as though employees reluctant to confront their own sense of powerlessness had displaced their fears and suspicions of management on to each other.

One morning I was cleaning up in the staffroom when the prime minister came on the television and I gave him a piece of my mind. 'No politics in the staffroom,' said a fresh-faced man in a powder-blue shirt. 'There's nothing wrong with an argument,' I said weakly. He was so full of himself I thought he was a manager of some sort. You couldn't get away from them, even in the staffroom. 'You'd lose,' he said. The murmuring of other voices ceased. I felt my face burning but said no more. I rushed out to the loading dock and was relieved to see Sally, who had a larrikin streak that was a tonic in the atmosphere of the Club. She had been there two years, but chafed against its constraints. In any case she pronounced Blue-shirt unique, saying that he was the only employee to have risen to a position high above the one he started in.

But he was far from the only one who seemed to conform to what the members expected. You heard hints of the deal if you spoke out of place. 'You can't have an opinion in the workplace,' said a friendly 30-year-old receptionist who seemed to think I was headed for trouble. I doubted I would be sacked for speaking out of turn. I had the impression that it didn't much matter what you said, as long as you were obsequious enough for your words to be ignored.

I asked a member who commented on our prices if it was very expensive to belong to the Club. He nodded. 'How much?' I asked, but he didn't reply. I was starting to break my own rules.

When I accepted the job in the Buffet, I had made a deal with myself that I would put up with whatever the other employees put up with because they needed the job. I could stay in the steamy nook at the back of the kitchen for hours on end slinging scalding saucers and sandwich plates from rack to stack, wincing a bit because my fingernails had developed an infection and my fingertips were burned, but I couldn't hold myself in any longer. The stifling atmosphere of the place was getting to me. A federal election loomed, and I felt compelled to draw attention to it. With election day only a week away, I asked a member ordering a latte how he planned to vote. 'Liberal, of course,' he said.

From that day forward, I asked the question whenever I dared. 'That's not nice,' said a barman who overheard me. I gathered that my venturing into the deep waters that swirled around the members' interests made my fellow employees nervous.

When Sally broached the subject of politics, she stuck with the mechanics. You could get off work two hours early to go and vote, she told a waitress. 'They make you vote for something every five minutes,' the waitress said crossly. The politicians were lucky that voting was compulsory, judging by the contempt for the process shown by my co-workers. They weren't the only ones. The election was held on a Saturday, a day when we saw some of the younger members at the Club. I found them a little bloodless, on that day in particular. 'I hate voting,' said one. 'They push all those things at you,' said another. I ought to be careful, the barman who had warned me before told me. Some of the members were high up in the Liberal Party. One might have assumed that much. But there were conservative voters on both sides of the counter. 'How *can* you, Antigone?' I asked a waitress of about 60 who often did the breakfast shift. 'You're a working woman.' The very phrase annoyed her. Like politicians courting the so-called aspirational voters, Antigone seemed to think that class was a dirty word – even in a setting where uniformed attendants were encouraged to grovel to the people they were serving. 'I work for myself,' she said crossly, redefining her menial position as one over which she had some control.

But it was the absence of control that I kept noticing. The things that had to be done each day filled the morning, but once the rush at lunch hour was over and the dishes had been washed, the afternoon seemed to stop in its tracks. Jill was right – there were days when we had little to do but stand around for hours. They were the worst, ripping a hole in the fabric of the day, the sense of lethargy pressing you down, though you had to stand poised even if there hadn't been a customer for hours. Because the Buffet had been all but deserted one week, we had done all the make-work we could. Lesley had polished the silver, Paula had bleached the cups, Estelle had filled bowl after bowl with white meat she stripped from cooked chooks, and I had been on my hands and knees two afternoons in a row, cleaning out the warming ovens and the fridges beneath the counters. There were more of Us than Them. Only for something to do, two or three of us would spring towards the counter at once to serve a single slow-moving member as Tina stood at the counter, writing things down. She jotted down anything out of the ordinary in her *Daily Report* book, an amazing chronicle of life in the cafeteria. There was a vintage sample of her work, on the back of the order form for a notoriously unstable member, stapled to a page of the book. 'Mrs . . . complained she had a heart attack two days earlier and went to bed and the doctor didn't come.'

I had been rostered to work for eight days straight. The prospect filled me with horror. 'You might have to work ten days straight,' Jill replied, when I said something about it. I didn't have the presence of mind to remind her that she had promised me the same two days off each week so that I could go on doing other jobs. The next day we were flat out at lunchtime. I made a member a roast turkey sandwich and gave it to him without adding the usual sprig of parsley and squishy half-tomato. It was a serious oversight. The moment the rush was over, Tina followed me to the back of the kitchen, holding a plate on which she had arranged four crusts, a sprig of parsley and a bit of tomato. 'It doesn't look so lonely,' she said.

After more than a month at the Club I was ready to quit and I gave Jill notice the following day. She didn't seem surprised. The Club clearly had a steady turnover of employees who found themselves unable to cope with its stifling atmosphere. 'If it's not for you,' she said briskly. Since I was on probation, if I liked I could leave right away. I gave it one more day.

Lesley was off work that week. Janet would soon quit herself. But the others reacted with disbelief when I told them I was leaving. One or two tried to convince me I was making a big mistake. 'Why?' Anna, the chef, asked gloomily. 'This is a *good* job.'

Chapter 2

THE FACTORY

CLEARLY, IF I WAS serious about trying to get by on a minimum wage, I'd have to leave Sydney. I picked the thriving agricultural town of Greendale, as I'll call it. A union official had told me that it had 1 per cent unemployment; *anyone* could find work there, she said.

I left home in early January. The bushfires in parts of the state had thickened the air and turned the sky a sulphurous grey, but the sky over Greendale was a piercing blue with picture-book puffs of cloud. That endless blue would become menacing after weeks without a drop of rain; for the moment, though, the world itself seemed suffused with potential.

I didn't know a soul in Greendale and was exhilarated by this at first. I revelled in the idea of making a fresh start, like a drifter blowing from town to town. Indeed, I *was* starting from scratch. The calls I had made beforehand hadn't yielded any useful information. Employers said to ring the employment agencies. The agencies said they could always find you *something*. This seemed to be a technique for bringing people desperate for work to the area in case there was a sudden demand for labour, which may be why it reminded me of the time my family emigrated to Australia. The consular officials who interviewed my father asked dozens of questions but were unable or unwilling to answer his queries about life in Australia. Dad had hoped to buy a small farm – farming was the only life he knew – but someone he met in Sydney early on told him that the land was so dry you needed hundreds of acres and thousands of pounds if you were to go up against the big blokes. It nearly broke his heart. I guess no one told him about Greendale, where immigrants had been leasing and buying farms for decades and you still heard a mixture of languages on the main street – part of the everyday clamour of a town in which application forms for jobs sticking labels on bottles or cans asked which languages you spoke *other than* English.

Towards evening I checked into a motel in town, paying $60 a night for a mouldy room at the back. The view of the parking lot was thrown in gratis. Sixty dollars was said to be a reduced rate, but I didn't want to pay it for long. It would eat up my capital, the $400 I had in my wallet to keep me going until I found work. I'd forgotten to check out accommodation. Because Greendale was a country town surrounded by thousands of scrubby hectares of nothing much, I had assumed I could find a cheap place to stay. I pictured a shabby furnished flattette near an overgrown railway station. I didn't stop to think about bonds and lease agreements. I expected everything would just fall into place. Part of me rushes headlong into things. The other part brings up the rear, carrying cardigans, blankets and blockout (not to mention pillows, sheets and towels, dishes, pans, a coffee plunger, a Walkman with some tapes, books, notebooks and a borrowed laptop).

The agent I asked about furnished flats the next morning looked at me pityingly and called a colleague who handled serviced apartments. Three hundred dollars a week in the heart of the country and they were booked solid. You couldn't make money on furnished flats, said another agent, offering me her mother's lounge suite for $150 and adding that I could sell real estate if nothing else worked out. It was one way to avoid sharing a room at the dingy backpacker hostel or pitching a tent on the Greendale showground like the fruit pickers who came in their hundreds each year.

The list of 'budget accommodation' I had picked up included a motel where a single room was $322 a week. I investigated the other options, keeping the temperature in mind. It was 40 degrees that day. Thick stone walls had a certain appeal, but the appeal was difficult to discern in the cabins at the caravan park. The cabin rented out for $195 a week had three double bunks and a Besser brick ambience. I was five people short of making it worth my while. Nonplussed, I mentioned my laptop to Robert, the manager. 'I could put in a table,' he said.

The better cabins had fewer bunks but were rented out for $220, twice the rent of a couple of small, shabby flats I saw later. The flats would have done, if I'd turned up in Greendale with a trailer of furniture, but renting meant paying six weeks' rent in advance. If you didn't have the bond money or, like me, didn't know how long you were staying, you were reduced to the most improvident arrangements, spending more than half your income to rent lodgings on a week-to-week basis.[1]

Many towns were the same and the cities were worse. But the extremes of wealth and poverty really stuck out in Greendale. On the north side of town the houses had more bedrooms than people; on the south side, seasonal workers they needed but seldom saw slept in tents and used public toilets and showers.

Seen from another perspective, this was my real introduction to the world of the low-wage worker – and I baulked. I was ready to take the first job I was offered, but not the room that went with it. The room at the local pub, for instance. Like the barber shop in the nearby arcade with the shelf of Zane Grey westerns and the sign 'Traditional Australian haircuts' over the mirror, the musty hotel room with its single metal-frame bed, basin and sprigged wallpaper (toilet and bath down the hall) was unchanged since the 1950s. The rate had gone up from a few pounds a week to $150. But I had no sooner encountered the first sharp shock – the cost of decent accommodation in Greendale – than I gave up the idea of finding lodgings for less than half my pay, compromised on location location location, and moved into a bed-and-breakfast in Broadacre, as I'll call it, a nearby hamlet. For $200 a week, I had a suite of rooms and someone to talk to. Val, the proprietor, a dogged, capable woman of about 60, was born and raised in the area, which made her a good source on local attitudes and customs. I told her what I was doing and she set up a card table for my laptop in a room with a view of next door's cascading fixed sprinklers. Finding Val and her cottage was the day's one triumph.

I had spent the morning traipsing from real estate offices to employment agencies. The real estate agents were nicer by far. Though I couldn't have known it, my future dealings with the providers of labour market services would be exemplified by my experience at Acme Personnel, the first agency I visited. I recognised the name of the big blonde at the front desk. I had spoken to her when I phoned from Sydney. 'If you send a résumé,' she'd said, 'we might be able to get you a really good job – like permanent.' This was optimistic. Several years into the new millennium there were fewer permanent full-time jobs than there had been in 1990. But I expected she could help me find work of a more provisional kind.

'Hi, Jacinta,' I said. 'I'm Liz Wynhausen. I sent you my résumé.'

Jacinta looked at me blankly. 'We get hundreds of them,' she said. Acme seemed to be in the business of collecting résumés and amassing them in secret, like people who collect hotel towels. Jacinta didn't bother to go looking for my documents. She asked if I was on a pension or benefit and, when I said I wasn't, produced a fistful of forms for me to fill in. Her attitude may have been a consequence of official government policy. Since the breakup of the Commonwealth Employment Service the system had been geared to helping people under 25, the long-term unemployed, and pension and benefit recipients. Full stop. In a logical extension of the user-pays principle, the agencies didn't make much out of finding work for other job-seekers who walked in off the street, as I did – because finding them a job didn't save the government money. But the whole approach was a failure.[2]

I registered with three more agencies that day. None contacted me, though I dropped in again and again to see if they were as bad as they were reputed to be. They were. Senate estimates for the year to March 2003 showed that just 12.3 per cent of the most disadvantaged job-seekers who went through labour market assistance programs found full-time employment. In general, about a quarter of the people who found jobs were back on benefits in six months, with increasing numbers of them condemned to what Dr Iain Campbell of the Centre for Applied Social Research at RMIT has called the 'zone of intermittent employment'.[3]

THE FACTORY

I may be willing to suffer certain indignities, but it's beyond me to suffer them in silence. I had listed factories, wineries and fruit packing sheds on my list of job preferences, and at Riverland Personnel one day, I asked the young woman behind the counter why no one had contacted me about a factory job the agency was handling when I had been in only the previous day vigorously reminding them that I was still job-hunting. 'We're very busy. We can't ring everyone,' she said. But the office was empty. The other clients must have been visiting the so-called service providers up the street, seeing if the service was any better. I met one girl who expressed a preference for Riverland Personnel. I said it seemed to be the sloppiest and she grinned. 'That's why I like them,' she said.

The employment agencies in town were legendary for all the wrong reasons. People often repeated what Val had already told me – you could always find work, but you wouldn't find it through an employment agency. By making some calls myself, I had heard about a job on the weighbridge of a winery. 'See Mr —— on Monday,' said someone there. That left the weekend to fill.

I marched along country lanes (dusty tracks cut through paddocks infested with snakes) and came across a house that rose up in the fields outside town as a surreal vision of the fruits of success in Greendale. It was a sort of brick bungalow on steroids which locals pointed out as one of the sights thereabouts. The ornate gateway was off a dirt road that only heightened the sense of unreality as you glanced from the modest farmhouse and orchard on one side of the road to the massive stone pillars and pergolas on the other. The ostentation conveyed something of the special nature of the country towns that exemplified the shining success of Australia's migration program. Despite the roll call of Whites, Browns and Smiths on the pioneer memorial in the main street, the foundations of Greendale's wealth had been planted by olive-skinned immigrant farm labourers whose descendants had come to dominate the style of the town.

There were produce companies with offices down one end of the main street where the tantalising scent of fresh onion hung in the air. From the nearest hillside the orchards and vineyards spread out below were like pieces of parachute silk tightly wound around the town. When the temperature rose to 43 degrees (making me feel like my thermostat was stuck), I ventured into a local leagues club and started scribbling away in a notebook. Four matrons whose conversation flowed between English and Italian were playing gin rummy. 'Are you writing a book?' asked one. I glanced around the vast, largely deserted lounge uneasily, as if there were a risk of being identified and exposed. The greater risk was that I would soon fade into the background, like the roses on the hotel room wallpaper.

The weighbridge job had disappeared into thin air by the time I appeared at five past nine on Monday. The man I had been told to talk to had suddenly gone blank on the subject, reminding me of something my father had told me about his early days in Sydney. When he turned up first thing, with his thick accent, to apply for a job advertised in the classifieds only that morning, he would be told, 'Sorry, mate, the job's filled.' Something of the sort seemed to be happening to me. I happen to have a broad Australian accent. But in Greendale, some people said it was was easier to get a job if you spoke Italian. The application form that I insisted on filling in at the winery with the phantom job asked me my birthplace. 'Holland' was no help at all.

'Don't tell me that,' groaned the fat man behind the desk at The Co-op, the agency that handled seasonal work, when I told him where I was born. He seemed to suggest a bunch of Immigration agents would burst through the door if I breathed another word about it. I couldn't believe it. In a town practically notorious for its association with ethnics, I was being told to keep my ethnic origins to myself – not that it helped much one way or the other.

When people told you there was always work in the area, they failed to explain that the work was fruit picking. Some young backpackers who went fruit picking ended up in hospital looking like they'd been on the toaster, said Val, advising me to buy long-sleeved shirts from St Vincent's in case I was desperate enough to try it. I bought two shirts, fearing a rush of other desperate people. I had toyed with the idea of fruit picking when I began my project. I was born on a farm. I have no memory of the apple trees behind the picture-book barn or the black and white cows in the green fields (Dad was a cattle dealer, the cows were Friesians), but in the back of my mind, farm life was mixed up with the lost world of early childhood.

I had already misplaced some of my enthusiasm for the life of a farm labourer after hearing that pickers often camped where they worked, however; I misplaced the rest after a friendly shopkeeper in Greendale told me it was imperative that I pack three litres of frozen liquid in an esky before I set out to tie vines or chip melons for twelve or fourteen hours a day. Wages varied – I had been told by an Australian Workers Union organiser that good pickers could make as much as $400 a day, but many others made only $75 to $100.

There was no work at the packing sheds. I thought of packing as the softer option until I called in on a big, dusty shed a short drive from town. Little forklifts loaded high with big plastic trays buzzed about madly, like mechanical creatures in a horror movie. A crew of women was sorting and packing the melons – honeydews – that tumbled down towards them. The youngest was a girl of school age. The eldest, a wiry little woman with permed grey hair and a pinafore, who had to be 60 if she was a day, hoisted a big box of fruit she had just packed to plop it down on a conveyor. I wasn't sure I could do it, but it didn't matter – they weren't hiring.

I tried asking for work at local motels, but it was the wrong time of year for tourists. Feeling the first slight stirring of panic

THE FACTORY

as another door clicked shut, I noticed a Pizza Hut and dived through the entrance. Naturally I didn't expect to be hired instead of a kid of sixteen, then paid $7 or $8 an hour: it was embarrassing acting as if one came from some weird planet where they gave the McJobs to senior citizens, but I was ready to try anything. That's how I found out that Pizza Hut gave job applicants a normative test – the Team Member Readiness Inventory. The youth who handed it over led me to a corner of the restaurant, too far from the door to flee with it. The 67 multiple choice questions seemed to have been imposed on our colony of Pizza Huts and Kentucky Fried Chickens by company psychologists in Dallas, Texas. Most of the questions were no-brainers about your personality, repeated in different forms as if to say that it doesn't matter if you lie but be really consistent about it.

I presented myself as a crawler ready to inform on a fellow employee who had promised to come into work but was really going to another job. The guys in Dallas evidently believed that the first requirement for dishing up pizzas was a willingness to dob in one's fellow employees. What would you do if 'a restaurant employee tells you he has been taking home a few restaurant supplies because he feels the pay is too low?' I lied and said I'd tell him not to. I couldn't bring myself to say that I would turn him over to management, even in a quiz that exposed Pizza Hut's obsessive fear that employees paid peanuts were thieves and liars as intent on stealing company time as on robbing the corporation of 'mushroom, onion and olive mix'. I lied my head off and lied some more, answering the proposition that I would get along better with people if I weren't so argumentative with 'Definitely false'. I glanced guiltily around the empty restaurant.

The official part of the day over, I went swimming. I stopped on my way in to exchange a few words with Robert, the manager, a short, cherubic-faced man who seemed always to have a kind word for everyone. The swimming pool had just been refurbished, and Robert, who was immensely proud of it, was there twelve hours a day. I gathered he was a great believer in work. He seemed shocked to hear that I hadn't found a job. I was 55, I said a bit defensively, telling the truth about it for once, and he offered me the seniors' discount. This provoked me into pointing out that I was competing for jobs with minors who'd be eligible for the seniors' discount in 2038.

I went back to the employment agencies the next day. The only jobs they had were forklift driver and water truck driver, the drip behind the counter at Riverland Personnel said solemnly. Dealing with the agencies could give you the feeling that you had been hit on the head and started hallucinating. None had bothered to pass on the information that I could probably get a job at Chicken & Egg Enterprises. I'd gone back to an agency to fill in a form for C & E after Val had told me that the company employed over a thousand people in the region, most of them at the chicken processing plant at Barralong, a short drive from Greendale. The application form asked if I had ever been convicted of a criminal offence. 'Applicants are advised that answering YES to this question will not automatically preclude them from working at Chicken & Egg Enterprises.' You could probably get a job at C & E if you were still breathing – as long as you didn't breathe too deeply. 'Some people would only stay an hour,' said a woman Val knew who had worked as an egg collector in the days when there were thousands of chooks underfoot in a big old shed thick with dust and filled with the choking smell of ammonia.

I didn't hear anything from C & E until I called the company myself (and learned that the employment agency hadn't yet passed on my forms). The real news was that I wouldn't have to touch the chickens, dead or alive, a prospect I dreaded. Tamara in human resources said there were vacancies in the Egg Plant, where some 30 women and a handful of men unloaded, sorted, stacked and packed around 47,000 dozen eggs *a day*. I was immediately employed as a general hand, on a casual rate of $13.77 an hour, which would rise to $14.32 after three months' probation. The interview took ten minutes. Tamara asked why I was in Greendale and whether I wanted a casual or permanent job, an inexplicable question since the company was only hiring casuals. The whole division would be sold before long, not that Tamara mentioned it. She made a copy of my driver's licence (no one ever commented on the discrepancy between the date I wrote on the forms and the date on my licence), and told me to wear old clothes to work, bring my lunch with me and leave my valuables at home. I was shown over the factory after the interview one afternoon, and started work at six the next morning.

The machinery in the centre of the Egg Plant ran along three sides of a square. The eggs were unloaded on to a conveyor belt on one side. Suction caps plopped 24 eggs at a time on to spools, to be sorted by hand, washed by machine and sorted again under the lights of the candler. But activity was concentrated around the section of the machinery called the packer. When I was first shown around the factory there had been a few employees on one side regulating the mechanisms that filled the cartons with eggs, closed them and pressed down the date-stamp stickers. On the production line on the other side, seven or eight women were packing cartons of eggs into boxes of various shapes and sizes. Few did more than nod grimly when I was introduced. They didn't have time for socialising. The cartons jiggling towards them all but flew from the machine and up each chain. I soon learned that the computer-set speed of the packer might be edged up a notch at about 3pm, not long before work ceased for the day, pushing the workers to the limit and leaving them to recover in their own time.

Towards the end of my second day in the Egg Plant, I stood at the packer desperately grabbing the 700-gram cartons of Generic eggs and packing with both hands (the only way to go fast enough) – as I had been taught by Mandy, the woman assigned to watch over me until the trainer had finished with another 'new girl'. The women on either side of me were packing, stamping and initialling the boxes, moving from station to station so rapidly that a documentary of the scene would have looked as if the film had been speeded up. I tried to keep up. I couldn't. My body had stopped following orders. My hands hurt, my arm was bruised, my back ached. 'Don't panic,' Mandy had said more than once, but I was beset by panic. The contraption that pressed the cartons shut wasn't working properly. Suddenly a phalanx of open cartons came bouncing towards me, the whole lot going awry so that one carton levitated as the rest started bumping each other sideways. Eggs burst out of the boxes and broke on the takeout chain. The sight filled me with terror. '*Mandyyyy,*' I wailed.

Mandy was a woman of formidable size with a voice that could have shattered china. I went home at night with her voice ringing in my ears and was grateful – I needed her help constantly. I had the greatest difficulty, for instance, in assembling the grocery boxes the eggs were packed in. Square boxes had flaps which had to be interleaved. I was slow to figure it out and even slower to contend with the boxes that had to be taped top and bottom. It looked easy enough when someone else did it, snapping off the end of the tape with a deft flick of the wrist, but I couldn't get the knack, and ended up with tape all over me, struggling with the dispenser as if I were in a Buster Keaton film. Whatever else was happening, the cartons of eggs kept rocketing out of the packer and up the chain at the same inexorable speed. Welcome to the industrial revolution.

I hadn't expected to show aptitude for the work. I was never any good with my hands. But aware that I seemed sort of pathetic to Mandy, who was half my age, I felt some urge to explain my clumsiness. I hadn't worked on a production line before, I told her. I wasn't used to the relentless speed of the machine. 'You *never* get used to it,' she said. Mandy could hurl a heavy stack of the cardboard for the boxes on to the shelf above her head without blinking an eyelid. The others did the same thing, but it was Mandy's physical strength that was most noticeable because of her boisterousness and bravado. She needed to assert herself in any exchange with her co-workers, as if ordinary working life presented her with battle after battle for supremacy. 'What are you fucken talken about?' might mean no more than 'Beg your pardon?' but Mandy wasn't a 'Beg your pardon?' kind of person. I hadn't been in the factory more than a few hours when she decided that someone further along the production line was talking about her. 'Don't fucken trust anyone here. They'll stab you in the back,' she said, repeating the sort of warning I had already heard in the rarefied atmosphere of the Club.

Mandy had worked in the factory for three years but said she still went home every night with her body aching. Rather than blame the work practices, or the fact that she and her co-workers spent up to ten hours a day, *up to six days a week*, in a hard, dirty job no one ever praised or thanked them for, Mandy found other ways to express her feelings and other people to blame. She wouldn't work at Hendersons, 'not for anything,' she said. Hendersons was a big food processing plant fifteen kilometres away. I had driven to the plant, only to learn that all the people on the factory floor were contract workers taken on by a labour hire firm. 'I wouldn't work there if you paid me. They're all Indians there,' she said, insisting that immigrant workers took jobs from 'Australians'. I had heard people in Greendale say something of the kind about C & E a moment before making it clear that they would as soon pass through the portals of hell as the entrance to the company's chicken processing plant, up the road from our factory. A real estate agent who asked what I did for a living failed to ask me another thing – not even if I was interested in the cheap and nasty flat she had shown me. Thousands had been employed by the company at one time or another, but working on the production line at Chicken & Egg Enterprises was still about as low as you could go.

Work began when the bell rang on the stroke of six, though employees generally clocked in ten minutes earlier, after trudging from the dusty parking lot past the grain mill, truck depot and engineers' workshops to the small tearoom next to our factory, where they would sit in the same place at the same table each break every day. The tearoom was rank with the smell from the nearby chook sheds, but you had to sit somewhere – if you were new, that was easier said than done. The first three hours of the working day lasted longer than eternity, then there was a bell for smoko. On my first day I trailed after Mandy, and sat down at her table in the tearoom. 'That's where Helen sits,' she said, and I jumped up again.

The first day in any workplace is fraught, and walking through the tearoom was like running the gauntlet. It reminded me of an incident I hadn't thought of in years. One day when I was ten or eleven, wandering through a patch of scrub on the way to the beach near my home in Sydney, I came across some older girls standing together in a little clearing as if waiting for someone. I ran away as fast as I could. I no longer remember if they had threatened me. There was no reason to expect anything sinister would happen, but I saw something in them that I hadn't come across before and I was terrified. They were implacable.

That was what I recalled as I scanned the tearoom for somewhere to sit down and looked into one set face after another. It was as if the harshness of the working environment had imprinted itself on workers who had grown up in the area. I could smile eagerly all I liked. Nothing I did or said would soften them. The outsiders were friendlier – if they dared. When lunchtime rolled around, a tired-looking woman who had talked with me for a minute when the packer stopped, saying she had been in the factory two months and hated it more with every passing day, walked up and pressed a two-dollar coin on me because I didn't have change for the soft-drink machine after leaving my purse in the glovebox of my car. But she was from a town hundreds of kilometres away, rather than

THE FACTORY

Greendale or the surrounding hamlets where the sullen mistrust of outsiders was like a defect they were born with. Local people didn't bother with civilities. You were as likely to get a hard, unblinking stare as a greeting, especially if you came face-to-face with the supervisor, Shirley, a short, belligerent woman who hadn't been in the job long and stumped around like someone looking for a brawl.

When Shirley came barrelling through the factory one day shouting my name, I was sure she was about to fire me. Mandy had told me more than once that I'd be sacked if management found out I had lied about my age (which I had confided to her, feebly hoping to win her over). But Shirley merely produced a piece of paper from human resources. 'You've got training tomorrow,' she shouted over the clatter of the machinery and the beeping of the forklift.

Shirley and I hadn't exactly become acquainted. On my first day, complying with company rules, she had leafed through a book that spelled out company policy on everything from occupational health and safety to 'media policy'. 'What's media policy?' I said – I had to ask. 'You never talk to the media – never ever,' said Shirley. We were in her tiny glass-walled office, our heads bent over the company manual, ticking off the rules with which I was supposed to be familiar, an empty procedure that took twenty minutes. Shirley didn't waste a second of it asking me if I was getting on all right in Greendale and whether I had found a place to live.

I quickly fell into a routine, driving home in the heat of the afternoon to shower, nap, and work on my laptop for some hours, noting down anything I remembered, before heading back through Greendale to the pool, for the half-hour it took me to swim a kilometre. I had taken up swimming the year before and was glad I had. Without it, my back and shoulders wouldn't have stood up to the hard physical labour. I was stiff and sore, nothing more, but I couldn't have been more relieved to hear that our nine-hour working days were to be cut back to eight. The hours reflected the patterns of an industry shaped by the laying cycle of battery hens killed after about twelve months spent crammed into cages. My co-workers must have known what was coming when Shirley called a meeting, but they reacted to the news that they would shortly be starting work at seven in the morning with seething, half-suppressed anger. When production was stepped up again, in three months' time, they would have to work ten-hour days with six o'clock starts.

'We're starting at seven,' said Shirley, standing like a boxer with her feet apart and her shoulders hunched, across from the employees perched between the cartons on the conveyor belt. 'Has anyone got a problem with that?' A sea of hands rose in the air but that was the extent of their protest. She took no notice. 'From next Wednesday we're starting at seven in the morning,' she said.

'*I'm* not,' said the grizzled maintenance man, who was the

THE FACTORY

union representative and didn't mind who knew what he thought of management. The others just muttered about the decision when they reached the tearoom. They challenged each other automatically, but little in their experience suggested they could reason with management. I had already heard as much from Mandy, after commenting on the heat inside the factory. 'You could be out in the sun pulling dead chooks out of cages,' she said. 'If they tell you you're out on the farm, you go or you lose your job.'

Though the company needed a constant flow of employees, my co-workers believed they would be sacked if they stood up for themselves, and failed to do so even when the boss told them the factory was being sold. They certainly had no job protection – all but a handful were casuals. Those employed years earlier had been offered the choice of joining the permanent staff but generally chose not to – the permanents earned a couple of dollars an hour less than the casual rate for farmhands, the $14.32 per hour that came without any benefits – casuals didn't get sick pay or holiday pay and they weren't guaranteed constant employment. But for the nine months of the year that egg production was at its peak, they got to work 50 to 60 hours a week.[4] The overtime kept them there. Working 60 hours, including overtime – at $20.33 an hour, if you were paid as a casual – meant taking home more than $700 a week, but going home hurting every night. It was a Faustian bargain. For three-quarters of the year, they worked until they dropped. For the next few months, casuals took home $380 or less a week, permanents even less, but they could give their bodies a slight respite. An employee-financed recovery period, you might call it.[5]

Because I hadn't worked in a factory before, the first thing I noticed was the absence of autonomy. You walked into the factory, found your name on the roster and went to your assigned spot. Four times out of five you were on the production line, rotated between packing and sorting eggs in 40-minute bursts that alternated the back-breaking labour at the packer with the concentrated effort of candling and sorting – staring fixedly at the eggs rolling past on spools, pouncing on the cracked and damaged ones, and removing them – which is harder than it sounds when 240 eggs roll past each minute.

Sometimes, at the start of a shift, people stood about chatting for a few minutes before the machinery was moving smoothly, but that was the only lull. Unless there was a brief mechanical hitch, you worked without stopping for three hours (the three hours before breakfast, if, like me, you couldn't swallow food at five in the morning), then had a fifteen-minute break, before the bell summoned you to the next three hours of hard labour.

On my third morning at work, Mandy materialised in front of me, her fresh pink face almost luminous over the white rubber apron she wore, and told me to find an apron and gumboots. We wore our own clothing in the Egg Plant. 'Wear clothes you don't mind getting wrecked,' Tamara had warned me, and I rapidly saw why, since I went home every day with my shorts and shirt looking like a Jackson Pollock painting done with yolk drips. But now, it seemed, we were to be drenched as well as spattered. The eggs came from the farms on coloured plastic trays that were washed before they went back to where they had come from. We were to spend that morning (the longest morning of my three long weeks in the factory) loading and unloading the machine in which the trays were washed. I took one look and shrank back. I used to pride myself on my fearlessness, another illusion shattered as soon as I was surrounded by machinery with moving parts. I was frightened of getting a hand or finger caught in something, frightened of not skittering out from under the forklift in time, and now that I'd seen the tray wash machine, I was terrified of slipping, falling and damaging my back forever. Soapy water poured from the machine, and I was in gumboots a size too big, stepping on and off pallets with heavy loads of plastic trays in my arms.

The first time I bent to pick up a stack of the trays from a pallet, my body refused to cooperate. Deciding I wasn't in Mandy's league, I retreated to the other end of the machine to fling back the trays still coated with egg or eggshell to be washed again and load the rest on to metal trolleys.

Then another woman joined me. Still in her twenties, Debbie had just been transferred to the Egg Plant on 'light duties': after three years in the boning room at the processing plant, the pain in her hand was so bad she had undergone an operation for carpal tunnel, an overuse syndrome fairly common in the industry. But

Debbie confided that she came to work to get away from the house. Her boyfriend, staying home on holidays at the time, played video games day and night. He didn't talk to her but he kept an eye on the children – that was why she stayed with him, she said, as we flung stacks of trays down on the trolleys. However bad he made her feel about herself, he was steady, unlike her own mother. 'My mother used to leave me with anyone, she didn't care,' she said, making it clear to me, a complete stranger, that as a small child she had been left with people who molested her. It was obvious that she was in a bad way but this was no time to talk about it. Mandy was advancing on us. She had reached into the machine while it was still going, managing to wrench her shoulder, or so she said, before wandering off to give herself a break on the other side of the factory.

'You've got to go faster or you'll get into trouble,' my new friend Grace whispered at smoko, stealing over soon afterwards to help. It wasn't the first time she had helped me out. Grace had come to my rescue on my first day at work, pointing out a spare seat in the tearoom, and we were soon comfortably acquainted. Grace was about 40, with short, curly dark hair and an intense, slightly jittery manner. She had followed her boyfriend to Greendale, reluctantly taking the job at C & E, the only one she could find. But she despised the place; like most of the outsiders I talked to about it, she had painful memories of her first days there. 'The machinery didn't scare me – it was the people,' she said when we went out for a coffee after work one week. I went in my stained work clothes without giving it a thought. Grace changed first. She said the townspeople looked down on C & E employees and showed it. A sales girl in a local dress shop had made a perjorative remark when she tried on something expensive, according to Grace.

Though she still felt isolated three years after she first arrived in town, Grace had one good friend at work. Jean, a former seasonal worker in her fifties, had landed in Greendale after roving all over the country with her partner and children. Rather than dwelling on the hardships of the life, Jean would talk about the highlights, like the camping spots they had had to themselves, as if the bush, the tree-lined creeks, even the night, belonged to them. Her optimistic presence was enough to restore one's faith in human nature. If there was one thing she admitted she wanted, it was a place of her own. She was stuck with her former partner until she saved enough money to rent a caravan, a mission taking an inordinately long time. But Jean never complained. Slender and sprightly, with ginger hair and freckles, she had the capacity to make the best of everything, even managing to give our workplace a bit of colour if there was a reason to celebrate. She brought in balloons and streamers before Australia Day, and she and Grace festooned the dreary old factory. The decorations were gone on the day, however, which meant the festivities fell flat.

Only one or two others did anything to dispel the grim, rancorous atmosphere of our workplace. If ever I recall scenes that typified life in the factory, this is one: my co-workers in the tearoom for smoko that Australia Day morning, seated in the same places, talking only to the people at their own tables, the one sign of anything out of the ordinary being the paper plates piled with scones and sweets that Grace and I had provided, which most ate without comment, as if the smallest spark of careless conviviality might be mistaken for weakness.

My two new friends were absent because they'd been instructed to go egg collecting. I asked about it the moment I saw them. I had decided to leave C & E early if I was ordered to spend a day at a farm. Research be buggered. No one could compel me to pull dead chickens from cages. You didn't have to touch the dead ones if you were only there for the day, Grace assured me. But handling live birds hardly seemed an improvement. Grace had spent the day giving them injections and ended up with a rash from the ammonia (in the shit that naturally flew everywhere when you grabbed a chook from behind and gave it a needle). But it could have been worse, she said philosophically. The first time she went egg collecting, she saw something in the cage that made her shriek in terror. 'This egg's got eyes and they're closed,' she told the first person who ran over to find her transfixed with horror at the sight of a dead white chook with its head in amongst the eggs.

At the end of my first week, I went to training with a bunch of other raw recruits, including a young Samoan soon to be a chicken catcher like his father, and a teenage girl who had just left KFC to work in the C & E processing plant. While I was relieved to be paid to sit down, others reacted as if the training reminded them of everything they most hated about school – at least until there was a bomb scare notable for the fact that the evacuation procedures detailed in the training manual ('remove in an orderly fashion to nearest exit') played no part in the mad flight from the building. Someone had telephoned the company to say there was a bomb in the processing plant. I had been worrying about getting trapped in the machinery, when the real risk was of being blown to bits by a disgruntled ex-employee or chook liberationist. Fortunately, our factory was a kilometre from the processing plant, which was the real centre of the empire – and the focus of the training in the occupational health and safety manual we were ordered to study.

The manual wasn't necessarily the best guide to daily life in the factory, however. I could just imagine what Shirley would say if I followed the order in the manual and advised her that the slippery floor around the tray wash machine was a workplace hazard. What you saw from the vantage point of the shopfloor was a system based on hypocrisy and deceit, represented by the gap between official policy and practice. Like the gap between the unenforceable toughness of the OH & S regulations and the number of inspectors employed to police them. (In 2004 there were 350,000 businesses in New South Wales and 301 inspectors – the 301st being the director of the

Occupational Health and Safety Division. The other 300 each had to inspect 1500 workplaces a year, at least in theory.)

In the factory the following Monday, I was on tray wash again. This time it was with the trainer, Sylvia, a flinty, fair-haired woman of about my age, who began by producing another manual with 100 or so pages describing how to operate the tray wash machine. 'It's the law,' she said shortly. Sylvia was annoyed by my questions, but, fancying herself a bit of a psychologist, she made bleak pronouncements about human nature. She didn't think much of it. 'People are vicious,' she said once, gloomily suggesting that I couldn't trust anyone I worked with. Since I was the one who was going home to take notes, I rapidly changed the subject.

I would head off to town to swim after working at the computer, get back around nine in the evening, snack on cheese and biscuits, make sandwiches for breakfast and lunch the next day, work at the laptop a little while longer and then fall into bed gratefully, in time for the eleven o'clock news. Since I didn't have time for a social life, I told myself that it was fortunate I had none. But I had never been as solitary as I was in Greendale, not even when I was first in New York on my own, many years ago.

The isolation weighed on me most heavily at weekends. After I had worked at the computer for a few hours, I would comb through the local paper a little forlornly, looking for diversions. Saturday mornings weren't too bad because there was a farmers' market where I went after my swim, before going home to make

THE FACTORY

myself an omelette for lunch. By four in the afternoon, however, Greendale looked as if a small neutron bomb had gone off, leaving the cars and buildings intact but vaporising the people. It made me feel a little desperate for human company. Although I don't like country and western music, I drove 37 kilometres in the beating sun one weekend to a town where the local club had a show by a country singer called Rodney Vincent, whose proud boast was that he had once been a support act for Gene Pitney.

When I was first in Greendale, without so much as the name of another person to call on, unless you counted the big blonde at Acme Personnel, I tried to find like-minded people. I left a message for a woman from a local book group I had heard of at the public library. She didn't return the call. She may have been away on holidays, I told myself. People were friendly if I walked into a shop to ask for directions or spoke with them at a club, but the friendliness was superficial. If they were locals, they kept to themselves.

It wouldn't be right to say that no one asked me out. My gregariousness was sometimes misunderstood. A shopkeeper in the main street, who said he was on his own now, asked if I liked ballroom dancing. I had two left feet, I told him. 'Pity,' he said.

'How are you fixed for tonight?' a friend of Val's, a leather-jacketed bikie who had to be 60-something, called to ask one evening. The prospect of romance twinkling on the horizon was as unexpected as it was unwelcome.

But that was it, socially speaking, until Grace and I went out for a coffee. The whole time I was in Greendale, only three other people even noticed my comings and goings, and one was the manager of the swimming pool. I thought the lack of social interaction might be a function of my age, until I talked with a young woman working behind the bar at the leagues club who complained that the local people never asked her to join them. I hadn't spent any time in leagues clubs before, but drawn by the air-conditioning and the abstract idea of company, I had become something of a regular. On Friday nights the lounge was full. You could be part of the crowd for the couple of dollars it cost to buy three raffle tickets (for a meat tray from which I averted my eyes) and another $1.30 for a lemon, lime and soda. This was just as well. My wages wouldn't have allowed much extra in the way of entertainment.

For the first four days, including the training day, the company paid me $474.30 gross for 30 hours at the normal rate of $13.77 and three hours at the overtime rate of $20.33. The tax was $137 because I had nervously insisted that I wasn't eligible for the tax-free threshold. I had the superstitious idea that I would get into trouble with the Taxation Office if I claimed it, which meant I pocketed $337.30 for my first week on the job. By the time I had given Val her $200, bought petrol, paid entry into the swimming pool, picked up some newspapers, and bought groceries at the supermarket and fresh fruit and vegies at the farmers' market, I had $7 left. I had $17 left the following week when I pocketed $353.80 for 36 hours and eight minutes' work.

I had had my old car serviced and repaired before driving to Greendale, paying the $630 bill from the garage out of money I had put aside. I couldn't have managed otherwise, with or without the tax-free threshhold. I might have cut back a bit on the supermarket bill, I suppose. I bought fresh asparagus and canned artichokes on a cabbage soup salary, but I don't smoke or drink, I took sandwiches to work rather than buying canteen food at C & E, and I bought nothing else but handcream, bandaids and an anti-inflammatory cream from the chemist. I didn't mind trying to live just on my wages. What bothered me more was the oppressive isolation.

I had counted on feeling a connection with the hard-pressed people I worked with. Instead I felt surrounded by hostility. One morning I broke every rule in the book and gave several of my co-workers a spray. I had greeted them as we headed to the factory from the parking lot. When my greeting was ignored, I announced that I had never worked with people so disagreeable to outsiders. 'I think we're very patient,' said one. From their perspective they were expected to help the interlopers do a job stolen from a local person in the first place.

Word of my outburst spread, or so I gathered after Sylvia issued some bulletins of her own. We were in the candler, which was rather like being in a tiny, overheated photo booth with lights above, a mirror on the facing wall and a drop curtain behind you, except that the booth reeked of the burned eggs that had fallen through the spools to the hot mirrored surface covering the machinery. On the candler, leaking eggs were tossed into a bucket to be processed into pulp, shell and all. Eggs with fine cracks were 'beeped out' with a wand attached to the computer (which dispatched all the remaining eggs to different parts of the packer to be plopped into trays and cartons). It was okay if the eggs weren't too bad but if a batch of bad eggs came flying past I sometimes grabbed the wrong one. 'You aren't coordinated, are you?' Sylvia said calmly. She wasn't one to raise her voice. 'I get pins and needles in my hands,' I said, mortified. It was a recurrence of an old problem. I was waking in the middle of the night because my hands were burning. In the mornings they were so numb and stupid I couldn't do buttons up and dropped things. But Sylvia wasn't done yet. 'You can't work and talk,' she said. 'If you want to socialise, join a social club.'

The one woman in the factory who looked almost elegant in her shorts and boots, Sylvia would risk asphyxiation, shutting off the air vent in the candler, so that the breeze didn't muss up her hair. She needed to set herself apart from the other factory workers, and my confidence provoked her no end. 'I've met other Dutch people,' she said as we went to wash our hands at the basin near the maintenance man's little empire, with its raggle-taggle overflowing cartons of spare parts. 'Germans, too. They're arrogant.'

The lunchtime bell had gone. I had arranged to attend a union

THE FACTORY

meeting with Grace. It was held on the benches outside the canteen, in an area heavy with the rank, suffocating smell of the chooks. There were eight people, including me and the union rep, out of the 50 who worked in our factory and the small plant next to it. Rather than giving any sign of being discouraged by the small turnout, the union organiser, a stringbean of a man with lank, straw-coloured hair, gave a speech suggesting that he was always on the case. 'Youse don't know the things I do for youse . . .' he said, dropping the name of the millionaire owner of the company as if they were on comfortable first-name terms. This part of the performance was even more disconcerting in retrospect, when it became clear that the company was about to dump the workers. No one asked him what was happening to the egg division, which was rumoured to be for sale, not even Grace, whose spirit had survived three long years in our dispiriting workplace.

Work kept stopping and starting that afternoon because there was something wrong with the packer. The sudden quiet would be preceded by the bell. The first or second time it rang, to signal another halt in the proceedings, the leading hand, a big woman who always looked like she was busting out of her overalls, lumbered up and told us to look busy. There wasn't enough work for all the people standing there, but we weren't allowed to sit down. I did so once, not knowing, and caught stares from the women on the production line even before Shirley hurtled over and ordered me to get to my feet. 'You're not allowed to sit down,' she said. 'What if there's nothing to do?' I asked. Shirley shook her head. 'Someone from management might walk in.'

The machinery soon clanked to a halt again. 'Youse can pack Best eggs,' Shirley shouted at the women on the production line. The Best eggs were hand-packed. The chooks that laid them were fed something called 'vegetarian' meal, according to the sleeves we slipped over the cartons. There were all kinds of rumours around Greendale about the ingredients of the other kind of meal the chooks were fed. In the old days, people dropped dead farm animals off at the plant, said Val. Though those days were long gone, it would be a while before I consumed another egg, whatever it said on the box.

But I was thinking about something else. Bothered by the idea that no one in the factory ever went home with the feeling they had done a good day's work, I had asked Sandra, a little twig of a woman in a big flannel shirt, if people took pride in what they did. Sandra looked at me as if I were cracked. 'You just do it,' she said. 'Like a robot,' said the woman next to her.

I was sent back to training a few days later, and reached the training room just in time to see a graphic image of a microbe chowing down on something that looked like the slabs of meat they raffled at the leagues club. The trainer had produced a white cardboard poster, like a school project, with a display of foreign objects found in C & E chickens – from a string from an ice belt to hair, even a hairnet! 'Our quality department has been cut . . . It's the customer that finds it . . . if the people on the floor aren't doing their job,' she said, as I busied myself taking notes on the foreign matter that had been found in our section. The list included bandaids and rat shit. I had worn bandaids to protect my fingertips from the cardboard and couldn't swear that I hadn't dropped one with a little Betadine on it in a 800-gram carton of C & E eggs. There wasn't time to ponder the mindset of executives who were willing to leave quality control of the product on which their fat salaries depended to employees making $10- to $14-something an hour. The trainer also said that people who were sick should stay at home for a few days rather than spreading the infection or contaminating the product. 'If you're not casual, you get sick pay,' she said wistfully. Less than a quarter of my fellow employees were permanent and the numbers were plummeting.

There was one more day at work before the long weekend. I had never known a weekend longer. The nights were punctuated by the mournful howling of the dingoes a man in Broadacres kept caged up, giving him something over which he had total control. The days were hardly more satisfactory. Val's house was full of family members in town for a funeral. I felt I should disappear, but it was too hot for long walks or drives. I retreated to the lounge of the leagues club one day, and did something even more out of character the next: I went to church with someone I had met at the training course – a short, round Sri Lankan woman with heavy-lidded eyes and a wide, beaming smile who had made me promise to attend her

Pentecostal church with her. It was my one invitation for the weekend.

The church, in a tiny shopping centre between Broadacres and Greendale, was in a Besser brick hall adorned with a few bunches of plastic flowers. Maria introduced me to Pastor Bill, Brother Pete and various members of the congregation. They were shop assistants, farm labourers and factory hands who lived in the outlying hamlets or on the wrong side of town. The older women had crimped perms and print dresses that looked like Sunday best; the younger ones herded small children and carried babies in their arms. There were Fijians, Indians and Filipinos, but most were working-class whites, interchangeable with my co-workers at the plant. But unlike them, the Pentecostals couldn't thank the Lord enough. More intent on the tantalising promise of the next world than the torments of this one, they smiled so much they looked like they were on something, enveloping me in a slightly glassy-eyed warmth that would normally have alarmed me. But there was no mistaking their tightly focused zeal. The Pentecostals were famed for it (or so I heard later from a Catholic priest I know). What Pastor Bill's church required was not that you *did* anything, only that you surrendered your life to the Lord. If you did, He would provide.

People told me their stories, when we talked after the service. They had heard that Maria was starting at C & E. One man said his wife had worked at the processing plant, packing chooks, but the cold and the repetitive movements had damaged her hands until she could hardly move them. 'I was out praying one night and the Lord told me my wife was going to get another job.' His wife found office work, just as the Lord had said. You could only hope that faith would work miracles for poor Maria.

Maria had been at the plant less than a week when we were summoned to a meeting with the boss, Mr Brown, a grey-haired man with a short back and sides who spoke in a whisper, as if rationing his voice. He turned up just before smoko and started mumbling about selling the egg division to another company. They were negotiating, he said. More would be known by the end of the month. 'It's positive, very positive,' he added. A slight shiftiness in his manner seemed to indicate otherwise. It was clear that he was uncomfortable. C & E was washing its hands of employees who had worked for the company for years, but he was insisting that there would be jobs for them. Some 50 people worked in the factory and in the pulp division next door. They would take 'everything' with them to the new company, he murmured.

No one asked him how he could be sure that another company would protect workers' entitlements or feel the slightest compunction about dumping older workers, like the half-dozen casuals already in their fifties. Employees perched on the conveyor belt or stood meek and silent, just behind Brown. I had tried both positions and was still straining to catch his words, so I spoke up. 'We can't hear you, Mr

Brown,' I said, more politely than I speak to my editors. Before Brown could say a word, Shirley leaped down my throat, ordering me to move if I couldn't hear. Brown was getting rid of the egg division, and most of them with it, but rather than turning on him, she turned on me. None of the employees tackled Brown or asked him so much as a question, as if their relative positions in the world remained unchanged even as he cut them loose. I had understood the lack of confidence behind the hard exteriors, but seeing them standing mute in front of the boss was like seeing them stripped of all defences.

Brown was still muttering platitudes. 'It's not all doom and gloom,' he said. A millionaire many times over, he was instructing his soon to be ex-employees not to worry, because worrying wouldn't get them anywhere. (It didn't. The company that bought the Egg Plant, essentially buying C & E's valuable contracts with supermarkets, eventually set up a new factory in another town, by which time most employees had quit – or taken what jobs they could get out on the poultry farms or at the processing plant.) I found the whole thing astounding, but it was difficult to know what my fellow workers made of it. They were too busy toughing it out. 'He didn't say anything we didn't know,' said one. 'We'll have a year – or two,' said another as they trooped into the tearoom for smoko.

It was time for me to quit. I had been there almost three weeks. Resolved to stay no more than a month in any job, I brought my departure forward a few days because I was worried

I would permanently damage my hands, which were badly inflamed. 'I knew you wouldn't stay long,' said Grace (who left before the year was out, moving to another town where she now works part-time as a room attendant in a motel).

I gave notice the next day. I was transferred from the packer to the loader, where trays of eggs that had been trucked in were lifted on to the machinery which rolled them towards the production line. The empty trays were whizzed straight back. Someone like me, suddenly surplus to requirements, would stand there stacking trays, reaching out lazily if there were one or two eggs left on them, before lifting the stacks of trays on to the trolleys, then pushing them over to the tray wash machine. It was restful standing chatting with the men who were doing the unloading. I asked one, a former cane cutter, if he could live on $14-something an hour and he looked at me in astonishment. 'It's a lot better than the dole,' he said. The other man on the loader had been in Greendale several months. He had rented a caravan but didn't know if he was staying. Greendale wasn't to his liking. The local people were so alien, he said, that he and his mate had speculated that it must be something in the water. Minutes later, Shirley stormed over to prove it.

The cardboard trays suddenly bobbing along the loader signalled the arrival of a batch of hatchery eggs which had shells so soft that every tray had broken eggs stuck to it. I was too slow in retrieving them and the trays started buckling into each other. Eggs were flying around as if they had a life of their own. I hadn't realised that I was supposed to be dumping the eggs but saving the trays, until Shirley started shouting that I had tossed out trays with bits of egg still stuck to them. I didn't have time to do anything else, I said furiously, and she took my place. I had just failed the test. It took me a moment to realise that I didn't care. By then I was shoving the empty metal trolleys out of the factory, going at my own sweet pace, to stand outside listening to the muted sounds from the big chook shed opposite.

I had never before peeked in, because I dreaded seeing the birds cruelly penned up in the small wire cages hidden inside the picturesque wooden sheds. Beyond the sheds, closer to the road, were paddocks in which a few sheep grazed. The whole place was bordered by a creek lined with weeping willows, part of a reassuring picture of farm life shattered as soon as one looked into the sheds. The rows of cages seemed to stretch into the far distance. Each was suspended over a waist-high hillock of shit. The chooks I could see had patches of red-raw skin. They had rubbed off their feathers against the wire of the cages, but would stay there until they were killed. I hadn't wanted to look, but having seen it, I couldn't get the image from my mind.

I wandered back into the factory, shell-shocked, when Shirley told me that Tamara wanted to see me in the office. She wanted to ask me why I had quit. Family reasons, I said.

I had given two days' notice. Why not skip it if I felt like it, said Sylvia. 'You'll only be packing eggs . . .' Sylvia had been there seven years. I stayed the extra day.

Chapter 3

THE OFFICE

I DROVE TOWARDS THE inner suburbs of Melbourne down a long road lined with spice shops, Indian restaurants, halal butcheries, Lebanese pastry shops, Italian delis, and stores with plastic-wrapped furniture piled on the street. Big-beamed Africans and Muslim women in burqas picked over the bargains out the front of overflowing fruit and veg shops. I could have done without the tram tracks, which required constant negotiation, but Sydney Road, Melbourne, the vibrant thoroughfare that sliced the southern capital's northern suburbs in half, had almost everything else I wanted from city life – especially after a month in the country.

I had decided to go to Melbourne to find work in a big city where I would be forced to find accommodation and get out of my comfort zone – if not *too* far out. I had friends there I would stay with for a few days and could call on any time. I didn't want to put myself in a position where I would be as isolated as I had been in Greendale. But that wasn't the only reason I went to Melbourne. I had toyed with the idea of looking for work in Tasmania, to check out crap wages as far south as you could go without settling on an ice floe, but nearly nine per cent of people in Tasmania were out of work and the classifieds in the local rags yielded thin pickings. I didn't have time to try it out.

I had gone from Greendale back to Sydney, and two months had flown by before I packed up the car and hit the road. The one tip I had picked up from checking out the web was that no one bothered to list crummy menial jobs that paid twelve bucks an hour. I reached Melbourne and leafed through the classifieds without improving my prospects. The only thing for it was to go door-knocking again. I picked bustling Fitzroy, one suburb over from where I was staying, and headed north along Smith Street.

The maps defined the area on one side as Collingwood and the other as Fitzroy, as if the middle of the street was the line dividing old working-class Melbourne from latte-land. I passed a tailor, a seamstress, a body piercing studio and some beckoning cafes. I tried not to look in the windows. I had caught sight of myself in the mirror in a shop selling smart clothes. I was wearing a black-and-white striped jersey and black pants that had seen better days. I looked desperate enough for money to ask for work door-to-door, but it wasn't a look likely to lead to an offer of work in a fashion outlet store.

Smith Street was in rapid transition. There were still plenty of Goths, hippies and ferals about (as if they had been let out ten at a time), but one end of the street had fallen into the hands of the retail chains. Soon a variegated shopping strip integral to Melbourne's character would be nothing but an elongated mall.

By the time I reached the Nike store, I had said my piece over and over. The teenager stationed near the store entrance picked up the phone to ask for the manager, an unseen presence out the back. Could I be seen through some kind of peephole? Were they checking up on the girl in front of me as she flogged the notorious Nike brand? Just don't do it! The company had hit the headlines for employing children in sweatshops in Asia where workers earned the equivalent of two American dollars *a day*.[1] I tried to hand over my résumé. I doubted that anything would come of it – it seemed unlikely that they would employ sales staff old enough to remember when sport shoes were called sandshoes and who had all the fashion éclat of a flour bag – but I couldn't help thinking what a coup it would be to infiltrate the place. Despite the mounting evidence to the contrary, I hadn't entirely dispelled the romantic notion that employees thrown together to work for a big corporation will see that their last best hope is to show the company a united front. 'We're not accepting résumés,' said the young cashier, her voice as blank as her face. What effing difference would it make if they accepted it or not?, the old me would have let fly. The new me slunk out of there, the offending piece of paper still in my hand.

I had a coffee to steel myself for the moment when I'd have to pound the pavement again, going through the motions, courting almost certain rejection. I enjoy talking to people, even complete strangers, but like someone faced with an unexpected illness, I was suddenly confronted with the loss of power and prestige I was hardly aware I relied on.

That afternoon, the proprietor of a lingerie store, a tired-looking woman with a lined face, stopped putting swing tickets on cami-knickers, listened to my pitch and praised my initiative, assuring me that someone would give me a job. I was to hear other words of encouragement from shop assistants. The older ones would stop whatever it was they were doing and say something positive, pleased to find someone looking for work the old-fashioned way, like a relic of the days when the milkman and the bread van also called around. But the woman in the lingerie store was the first to do so that day, and my thoughts rushed on so far ahead that I saw myself at work – edging around display tables piled with last year's camisoles and nighties – before I had so much as handed over my résumé.

Rather than changing it to explain that I had worked a month here and a month there, and had a certificate of service from a posh club to prove it, I stuck with my basic cover story which suggested that I had done casual work as a cleaner and function waiter for the same employers for three years. This was to make me seem solid and dependable. The proprietor seemed to be doing the maths. We had chatted a while before she looked at the résumé, but she no sooner started reading it than something in her manner sagged a little, as if a bra strap had snapped. She promised to call if anything came up, but I knew she wouldn't. My résumé drooped like a dead fish from her hands.

Up the other end of Smith Street the harbingers of gentrification included a shop called Vegan Wares, which was wedged between a locksmith and a fish-and-chip shop. I passed by some cafes. The restaurant and bar work that had been the preserve of older working-class people now went, more often than not, to glamorous youth. But drawn by the hand-lettered 'Waitress wanted' sign in the window of a tiny bar, I invoked my time in the Club after all. I marched in to tell the owner, a beautiful Korean, that in my last job but one, I worked in the food business, serving sandwiches and making cappuccinos. I regretted telling the truth the instant she asked me to make some coffees on the decrepit espresso machine.

While she remained at a discreet distance with her face averted (like someone trying not to look at the scene of a car crash), part of me was wondering if I would have felt less self-conscious under the openly mocking gaze of a Caucasian.

I should have concentrated on her words instead. I couldn't remember if she had said cappuccino and skim latte, or latte and skim cappuccino. From the second I had started fumbling with the cups, I knew there was no way on earth I would get the job, but I had to play out the scene whether my hands obeyed me or not. It was excruciating. I burned my fingers even before I burned the milk. The slightly sickening scalded smell floated up to fill the bar. I got through the next minute or two somehow, but in my hurry to be gone, I would remember only that a man had emerged from somewhere out the back of the bar and stood next to the woman, the two of them nodding like a double negative until I backed out of the place.

There are people who are put in that sort of situation every day of the week – like the people getting Newstart, newspeak for the dole, who are required to record ten job searches every fortnight, sixteen in some cases.

I was ready to call it quits, but the sight of another 'Help wanted' sign in the window of a bakery prompted me to enter. The sign, I should add, was for an *apprentice* baker. I went in to see what would happen – and what happened helped to compensate for the rest of the day. The boss bounded from the back radiating positive energy, saw me, stopped dead, and paled under olive skin already dusted with flour. 'Anyone over twenty I've interviewed for this job is too old,' he said. I *was* over twenty, I admitted with a grin, agreeing that I probably was too old to heave big sacks of flour around for an apprentice

THE OFFICE

baker's wage. His relief palpable, the baker said: 'At your age, you should be kicking back and drinking chardonnay.' It was a rare moment in an unsatisfying day.

The acute sense of timing that had propelled me to Greendale to look for work in the first week of the year, when everyone was on vacation, had brought me to Melbourne right after Easter, when shops started laying people off for the winter lull. There would be no more interviews until August or September, said a fortyish clerk in a suburban Myers store, a day or two later, impatiently waving my résumé away, as if I should have known better than to turn up when casual employees were getting their hours cut.

One day I wandered around hotels in downtown Melbourne filling in application forms, then legged it through the beachside suburb of St Kilda, leaving my résumé at a Novotel overlooking the bay. I had stayed there once years earlier and had complained about something, a recollection that filled me with shame. I had already taken a vow never again to complain about trifles such as the speed of service. I entered the lobby stealthily, half-fearing I'd be recognised – *'She stayed here. She never stopped complaining'* – momentarily forgetting that a woman of my age is about as noticeable as the glue behind the wallpaper.

I had also applied for a job at the Windsor, a hotel I once wrote about for *The Bulletin*. I may have described its faded opulence in print, but I wouldn't be making its beds. 'All the applications we receive are of a very high standard and the decision is certainly not an easy one,' they said in the letter they sent politely turning me down, '. . . however we thank you again for your interest in the Windsor and wish you all the best in your future endeavours.'

Lowering my expectations, I filled in an application for suburban Safeways, my second Safeways in two days. I had completed a pile of applications by then, scattering documents through three or four suburbs. I had combed through the classifieds, posted an application mentioning the requisite honesty, reliability and outgoing nature specified for the job in one shop, and faxed letters and documents to others; none of the smaller concerns bothered answering, as if I had descended to a level where common courtesies no longer applied.

I was starting to feel desperate, as if I had come to a dead end. I don't know if this happens to other job-seekers with nothing but their willingness to offer, but when I started looking for work, I was convinced I would find something right away. Having set out with such inflated expectations, only to be reminded that the bright personality to which I attributed some of my success as a journalist wasn't enough to get me any further, I applied for everything from a job in a carwash to a job as a food service attendant in a church home. I wrote to the home saying that it would give me an opportunity to do something positive and beneficial for society, as if I were running for political office rather than applying to dish out creamed chicken and mashed potatoes. Doing exactly as recommended in training courses for the unemployed, I followed up, leaving messages for the human resources woman to show how keen I was, only to realise I had blundered when I heard her frosty tone. People applying for work as uniformed attendants didn't summon people like her. They just waited for weeks for them to move pieces of paper from one side of their desk to the other.

If I were really the person I claimed to be, my few hundred dollars dwindling by the day, I would have been left high and dry, appealing to charities like the Brotherhood of St Laurence to tide me over until I was eligible for government benefits.

I posted off six letters one day and eight the next, still marvelling that this was what was required of people applying for menial work, however disconnected the application process from the skills demanded by the job.

By poring over the classifieds in local papers, often the best source for the worst jobs, I had established that there were always jobs for women who cleaned other people's houses. If you looked at the wanted ads as closely as I had, you started wondering about charting the market economy's winners and losers with a points system that showed how many people in any given area cleaned other people's toilets for a living and how many never cleaned their own.

The emergence of a class of well-to-do working women seems to have produced its own antithesis – a servant class of poor migrant women working as nannies, cleaners and maids.

In their book *Global Women: Nannies, Maids and Sex Workers in The New Economy*, Barbara Ehrenreich and Arlie Hochschild relate the rise of the new servant economy to the mid-1980s, when some women in the West started to enjoy the fruits of feminism, even as poor women from the Philippines or Sri Lanka left their own children behind to work for minimum wages in the United States – or the UK or Australia – looking after other people's children.

An ad in the *Caulfield Glen Eira Leader* that caught my eye said, 'Cleaners domestic required. Only enthusiastic, reliable and happy persons – car essential.' I phoned to ask what the happy cleaners were paid, but the woman from the agency refused to discuss it over the phone.

Though I had expected to find work rapidly enough to move to nearby accommodation, after a week as a houseguest, I could no longer stave off the search for housing of my own. Naturally, the city possessed an infinite variety and under 'Rooms Vacant', a kind of afterthought in the classifieds in *The Age*, I saw a room for $150 a week, less than I imagined I would be paying for room *and bath*. The other $150-a-week rooms were in flophouse hotels, but this one was in a defrocked monastery converted into conference halls and student digs.

The woman who rented out the rooms made me think of the housekeeper in the Daphne du Maurier novel *Rebecca*. It may have been the ambience of her ivy-covered mausoleum. On a bright autumn morning, with Melbourne's diffident sun practically skipping out of the clouds, the place was as cold as a tomb. The wind whistled along the corridors of a building so forbidding I kept looking over my shoulder, expecting someone or something to materialise out of the gloom. But I nearly took the room. It had a single bed, a lumpy mattress and a hard chair. No monk could have wished for less. Pushing aside all thoughts of walking alone through the corridors late at night, I asked Mrs Danvers if she needed a deposit of some sort. I could have given her $150 and still had enough cash for a radiator and a desk lamp. I'd brought a hot water bottle from Sydney, if no clothes to speak of. But the room was booked for another week. The sunless cell available until then made the first room look like a suite at the Ritz. Bathroom down the hall. I felt I had been tricked. But the real reason I didn't take it was that I dreaded rushing through Mandalay in the dark when nature called.

The real estate ads certainly offered more in the way of furnished accommodation than there had been in Greendale. In fact, I saw the very thing, for $225 a week: a studio apartment in a building with its own gym on St Kilda Road, the grand boulevard that sweeps into the city. I couldn't picture myself getting on an exercise bike after a day of manual labour, and as it turned out, I couldn't rent the apartment without signing a three-month lease. An hour stuck in the south-bound traffic democratically distributing fumes through Kooyong and Toorak, the choicest blue-blooded precincts of Melbourne, and I was motel-hopping in St Kilda, a suburb of such antic variety that a five-minute stroll from a bus terminus right outside Luna Park led past Acland Street – poppyseed strudel central for Melbourne Jewish population – around the block to community gardens where people with purple-streaked hair and nose rings grew cabbages and strawberries. But St Kilda had many rattier precincts. The first room I saw, in a quiet residential street with hookers posted like hydrants, was in an apartment building with spidery cracks in the glass and stained ruby-red sofas they could have rented out for a homemade horror flick. I took one look and fled to the Waterloo Motel, my home away from home for the next six weeks.

Located half a block from St Kilda Junction where a couple of expressways intersected with St Kilda Road, which meant dodging through six lanes of traffic to get to a tram stop, the Waterloo charged $280 a week for a single room with a small desk, a small table, a couple of chairs, a double bed, a bar fridge and a microwave. The light poured in, making the room tolerably cheerful, if basic. The only signs of the motel's chequered past were the cracks in the bathroom door and mirror. I had managed to hotfoot it from an ex-monastery to a reformed hot pillow joint.

Brian, the manager, a big, broad-shouldered man with grey hair tied back, who looked like a Nick Nolte character, a reformed bikie cast as a cop, had tipped the working girls out when he took over the place. The girls had moved to another part of St Kilda (where the unhappily named Victorian government would soon fail in its attempt to regulate St Kilda's sex industry by setting up a sort of free-fuck zone).

The Waterloo, in contrast, was lace-curtain dull. Nick Nolte took care of that. I seldom saw so much as a flash of underpants in the hallways. The guests were backpackers, salespeople and tradesmen. The regulars included the men rigging a tower at a Melbourne racetrack. They had stayed before but wouldn't be staying again. The owners of the building were selling – in six months' time there would be one more apartment block and one less decent budget motel close to the centre of Melbourne.

I arranged to move in towards evening, and gave myself the rest of the day off, wandering through St Kilda towards a coastline so flat it struck me as a few cliffs short of the real thing. The neighbourhood's newest amenity was an indoor sea pool in a refurbished deco building where they charged $13 to get in, one more sign that shabby old St Kilda was being cleared out to make way for the winner class.

The suburb of Prahran petered out at the other end of my new block, on a section of Prahran High Street where the aura of raffish charm mingled with the smell of mothballs, old age and furniture polish emanating from the secondhand stores. You didn't have to hock your furniture to get into the local pool, but it was out-of-doors. More accustomed to indoor pools, with struts on the ceiling, I backstroked up and down the pool the next morning staring at the milkily colourless sky, a little disoriented by the abundance of nature.

Nine days had passed. I'd relinquished all hope of living on my earnings – the $280 a week rent took care of that – but I had to earn something or call it quits. Yet if I couldn't find a job in Melbourne, with an unemployment rate under six per cent, what hope would I have elsewhere?

Then it hit me. I'd resisted applying for part-time work, but a job for a few inconvenient hours a day was better than no job at all. I pored over the classifieds again, found an ad for a part-time cleaning job and called Bob as instructed. Bob asked if I was fit and I boasted about my swimming. 'You can go in the Veterans' Games,' he said cheerfully. Whether or not I was applying for a job almost anyone could have, Bob seemed to have decided that I was the lucky one.

That much became clear when we met towards evening in the basement of a building a half-hour drive from my motel, and Bob introduced the clean-shaven Turkish-Australian with him as my new supervisor. Mustafa was a middle-aged man of medium height with brown hair tipped with grey. He seemed nervous and didn't say much, but the barrel-shaped Bob was as cheerful in the flesh as on the phone. He waved away the documents I offered to show him, which meant that I was about to start working for someone who knew just two things about me: I called myself Liz and considered myself to be fit. I would get $13 an hour – $39 a night. In case I was thinking of keeping it all to myself, Bob warned me that I would have to fill in a tax declaration. Of course, I said, and he beamed again. I couldn't remember meeting a jollier man.

THE OFFICE

The formalities over, Bob described the job. I would dust desks, empty bins and vacuum, going from one side of the building to the other. I was sure to get a shock when I saw the size of the area I had to clean. There were two wings and both were daunting, he said. He was full of warnings, now that I come to think of it. 'You don't think about doing all of it at once. You divide it up, like your laps. You tell yourself you're going to do four and then another four . . .' He instructed me to call him if I had a problem with Mustafa, who blanched and begged me not to, whispering 'Mustafa look after you,' the moment Bob's broad back was turned.

I nervously eyed a trolley with a vacuum cleaner, dusters, garbage bags, and other bits and pieces tucked in a removable canvas sling, which was parked in the tiny storeroom where the cleaners picked up their gear. Bob plucked something from amidst the tottering piles of toilet paper rolls on the shelves. 'Here you are,' he said, pressing a tiny bar of hotel soap into my hand. A token of my employment, and, as it turned out, my only reward for my night's work.

I started the job for real a couple of nights later as a bunch of suits from B Block left through the back door of the building, passing the storeroom where my new colleagues sat on broken chairs under a broken clock, smiling in welcome. There were five, counting Mustafa, who sat at the side at a little broken-down desk, with some pieces of paper in front of him, not that there seemed to be anything to fill in. Less harried than he had been around Bob, he introduced his smiling wife, Satma, and his widowed cousin, Ayse, an older woman with a long mournful face who was dressed in black. Gulay, the youngest in the group, had a tubercular cough and huge black circles under her eyes. Mehmet, the oldest, was a small, silent, nuggety man with an expression of amusement on his creased brown face. He had worked in a factory, dyeing materials. Some employees got sick because of the chemicals, he told me. But at 70, Mehmet himself was spry. They all switched from Turkish to English when I turned up, but later slipped back into their own language with relief, as if it shaped itself better to their thoughts.

Ayse came upstairs to show me the ropes, going into the commercial side of the building to dust desks and ledges. It was hard to concentrate on what she was doing. There were people still at their desks. I found it strangely disconcerting. I had thought about the physical demands of the job rather than the difficulty of being inconspicuous. Bob had explained that the people in B Block worked for a big accounting firm, which was the sort of higher-order information that was bound to distract me from my duties. I was supposed to be flicking the duster around and emptying the wastepaper baskets into the garbage bag in my trolley before lining the bottom of the things with recycled A4 paper.

Strange as it seemed to be cleaning other people's offices, handling other people's garbage bothered me less than I thought it would. 'Put like this,' Ayse said more than once, pushing a wastebasket back under a desk. I thought of saying that I'd worked in offices – I knew that office workers liked to have things put back in the same place. But there was no way of explaining it without going into detail, and talking in English made Ayse self-conscious. But she revealed a little about herself, telling me she had been widowed in the previous decade. 'I have bad luck,' she said, as if the early death of her husband was only the last and greatest of the misfortunes that had befallen her. Ayse was 60. She looked older in her widow's weeds but moved briskly, practically diving under desks in the empty offices. If there was someone still at a desk, she waited on the other side of the partition silently beseeching them to say something to indicate it was okay for her to go in.

I didn't mind chucking out their discarded soup packets and dirty tissues, but it was hard for me to act as if the people at the desks breathed a different air from me. I had bounced into several offices to do my thing with the bins when Ayse carefully explained in her rusty English that if there were two or three people in an office, that meant they were having a meeting and I mustn't go in.

Bob was wrong about one thing. I wasn't daunted by the size of the building, because I didn't have the faintest idea where we were. One open-plan office looked the same as the next. If it wasn't that the bins had been emptied, I would have gone around and around, moving the dust on the desks from side to side. I couldn't remember which door we went in or if we went out the same way when we finished. There was a lobby between the two sides of the building. I had to clean both, as Bob had warned. The other side, A Block, was a health clinic. Mustafa, who waited for me on the other side of a set of double glass doors, led the way through the meeting rooms and along a carpeted hallway to the doctors' offices, suddenly dropping his voice as if the doctors were still there. 'This one here the head doctor,' he whispered. 'He likes everything the same way.'

I went in and out of a bathroom, the men's one, uncomfortable about going into the *wrong* toilet (after realising late in the piece that cleaners didn't get the luxury of gender). I didn't have to clean the toilets; someone else did that. I merely disposed of some more garbage, tipping out the used paper towels by shaking them from the metal container rather than touching them with my bare hands, which is what I was doing when Mustafa hurled himself at his trolley to get me a pair of surgical gloves. 'You know . . .' he said, gesturing around him, as if to say, 'Who knows what they get up to in a medical centre?' I had already assured myself bravely that I couldn't get a needle-stick injury from the little syringe caps I had tipped out from another bin, but I put the gloves on. 'Don't worry. Mustafa look after you. You have question, you ask him.'

One and a half hours had passed by the time I strapped on the backpack vacuum cleaner that was to be my companion for the rest of the evening. I was back in B Block searching high and low for power points, crawling under desks and wriggling along on my stomach as if playing Cowboys and Indians all by myself, to locate the only free power point for half a kilometre. But the real bane of my new existence was the cord, which should have been long enough to lead me out of the wilderness, but was so snarled up I longed for an assistant to untangle it, leaving me free to concentrate on the specks on the mottled beige carpet I hadn't vacuumed yet (insofar as one could tell).

I tried to work in sections, as Bob had suggested, rather than darting all over the place, which was more my style, but I still couldn't determine where any section started or finished. Until I reached the double glass doors and crossed over the stairwell again, I had no idea if I was on schedule. I still had to vacuum the interminable hallways and offices of the spookily empty clinic. I finished just as Mustafa appeared on the other side of the glass doors. 'Easy job, you see.' I was sweating and exhausted. I hadn't had a sip of water in three hours. Those people who went to the cinema carrying their own water bottles would have been dead of thirst by then. 'Easy next time,' said Mustafa.

When Monday rolled around, I reached the storeroom at a quarter past five. I would be working on my own, and coming in early was the one chance to chat with the others, who treated the fifteen minutes before work as a proper social occasion. But the conversation was constrained by language difficulties and an element of caution on both sides. I was under the impression that Mustafa and Satma stayed at home all day looking after their grandchildren, but it wasn't the sort of thing I could ask without sounding like a snoop from social security and we talked about the weekend instead. Satma and Ayse had been cooking for a big family party. What about Mustafa? Satma gave me a look. She could be a little satirical about the male half of the species but probably waited on Mustafa hand and foot. 'Kitchen no place for a man,' she said. While they were shopping for food at Victoria Markets I had been food shopping at Prahran Market, I said, to emphasise the normality of my life. I would have liked to know more about their lives, but there were many boundaries we didn't cross. I asked safe questions about the size of their families and where to do my laps when the Prahran pool closed for winter, but I made only cautious enquiries about what they did all day.

I had confessed that I came from Sydney, tacking on an old aunt in Melbourne to explain why I flitted like a butterfly from one city to the other, behaviour that suggested a chronic inability to settle. I didn't mention the motel, of course, but I had the feeling that my flightiness was a mark against me. Satma asked me if I'd go back. 'Stay a few months,' Mustafa said. I agreed and he said something rapid in his own language that may have been a reflection on the unreliability of the rest of the human race. The young man who cleaned the stairs hadn't shown up. 'Because I have soft heart and paid him, he doesn't come,' he said. 'Is that the way? No.'

THE OFFICE

Mustafa came with me to help out on the first part of my appointed round, then went to check on another floor, leaving me to commune with the duster, the trolley and the vacuum cleaner. One or two of the men who were still at work lifted their feet or rolled their chairs away for me to vacuum beneath their desks. But I had something to ask them. I had crammed my reading glasses into a bumbag with my wallet and car keys on my first night on the job. The specs had fallen out, but I had no idea where. If I kept the job for three weeks, I would just about cover their cost. 'I lost my glasses the other night – I wonder if anyone saw them?' I had to say it again before they realised I was addressing them. Then one said no, he hadn't, sorry; and one shook his head. 'Of course, I'm not sure where I lost them,' I said chattily. Silence. There were those who acknowledged with a kind word or two that a cleaner had skittered in, but most just went on with their work. If there was a kind of absence, like the hole in the ozone layer, in the space occupied by a middle-aged woman in a menial position, it was incumbent upon the cleaner to be more inconspicuous still. People who do the job for real, such as school cleaners, said when I asked them that the lack of acknowledgment bothers them more than any other aspect of the work.

I had realised on day one that the work would be too solitary to learn anything much about my co-workers. On day two I concluded that I was totally unsuited to the position. I could no more be unobtrusive than I could ascend to a higher order of being. I vacuumed another kilometre of carpet commenting only under my breath, but it was beyond me not to draw attention to myself. Confronted with an office with so much mud on the floor it seemed to have been specially tracked in to demonstrate a new carpet cleaning product, I spoke again – I couldn't help myself – and the balding man whose office it was looked about, frowning, as if the vacuum cleaner had developed a voice.

I had paused earlier in the evening to chat with Russell, the fellow who cleaned the toilets. He was a solidly built man with a modest way about him. He told me that he rose at 2.30 am every day to clean supermarkets, drove a bus in the daytime, then cleaned bathrooms in our building at night. He had done it for years. 'It's just the way I am,' he said. He had gone by the time I returned with the vacuum cleaner.

The deserted clinic made me nervous. I walked into a darkened office and almost walked out again, seeing little black bear eyes unwinkingly watching me from a basket filled with furry toys. There were files scattered about on some of the desks. I assumed they were patient files. I was getting into offices I shouldn't have been in under the prextext of being a cleaner. I resolved this ethical dilemma, at least to my own satisfaction, by behaving as if I couldn't read but had special compensatory antennae for dust, crumbs and litter. My antennae failed me, however.

'Come with me,' Mustafa said, rather ominously, when I showed up for work later that week. He rushed upstairs to a big meeting room in the clinic. 'That cup has been there four days,' he said, pointing to a paper cup under a table. How could I have missed it? I had vacuumed the room each night, sucking up enough biscuit crumbs to cater for the meeting all over again.

I was too rattled by my failure to think to ask how he knew how long the offending cup had been there. In reality, I had an unseen adversary. The complaint had come from the receptionist in the clinic, an obsessive-compulsive who had plastered stickers with her name, Veronica, on every pencil case and phonebook in sight. Veronica sat behind a glass pane I had failed to clean at first. No one had mentioned it, just as no one had mentioned the entrances on both sides of the ground floor, conceivably assuming that a cleaner would know that the Windex was hanging off the trolley for a reason. Veronica kept insisting the glass was still dirty. I thought of writing 'Get a life' on it the last night I worked, but contented myself with removing the 'Veronica' sticker from her Rolodex.

'It's the little things,' Mustafa said, when he returned to check on my progress. I took it to mean that it should be obvious the cleaner had been, leaving the place looking better, even if she had only moved the dust or smeared the germs around, filling the air with lemon-scented air freshener rather than the meaningful smell of disinfectant.

I had come to suspect that I was being lumbered with an unfair share of the work – a suspicion based on arithmetic rather than the tribal loyalties at play. By dividing the number of floors by the number of cleaners, I had deduced I was the only one cleaning a floor on my own. I could have allayed my suspicions by sneaking up to the other floors to see if their occupants produced more crumbs than the medical staff or more dust than the accountants, but given the number of keys on the string around my neck it seemed likely the doors would be locked. All I knew was that there were some jumped-up executives up there. One had trodden dogshit all over the office carpet, then left a note ordering the cleaner to get rid of it, an order that ripped through the veneer of respect that made Mustafa's three-hour-a-night job as supervisor tolerable in his eyes.

But I had troubles of my own. A wheel had fallen off my trolley. 'It's stuffed,' said the young auditor I begged for help. He seemed amused. Since I have a slight limp, my three-wheeled trolley and I may have looked like we were in a special class for cleaners. Certainly we were noticed for once. 'Where's the other girl?' said a grey-looking man in a grey suit, referring to my predecessor, a woman in her sixties. He sounded a little aggrieved, as if he had come to work to find the furniture moved around.

In the clinic I waved to Russell and dashed into offices along the corridors saluting the absent staff by name. The names were on the doors. *How are we tonight, Roberta? Not much garbage, I see.* Several more weeks of this and I'd be right round the bend, talking to the teddy bears as well. Deciding that the offices needed a good going-over, I wiped down surfaces and reached up to clean ledges, rather than frisking a duster over them, and, absurd as it may sound, was feeling pleased with myself as I dragged the trolley back along the hallway towards the stairwell, half the night's work done.

This reverie was interrupted when Mustafa caught sight of me and burst through the glass doors, leaving a set of fingerprints his receptionist friend would complain about for sure. 'Why you don't get another trolley downstairs?' he said sharply. I lost my temper, shouting that there *weren't* any spare trolleys downstairs. I made so much noise that Russell poked his head out of the bathroom he was cleaning. He had come to my defence another night, telling Mustafa that I had cleaned the glass just as I said. But I didn't need defending again. I'm not my father's daughter for nothing. Sometimes I picture Dad in my mind, watching a western on television. When the cowboys started to brawl, Dad would be up on his feet, swinging punches at the air.

When I had walked into the storeroom on my first night and seen the other women smiling in welcome, I had let myself dream of creating a connection that would sweep away the barriers between us. But this was asking rather a lot of fifteen minutes an evening. I hadn't realised that would be the extent of the social contact I would have with most of them. They used the time to make warm, inclusive gestures, insisting that I take handfuls of the homemade cakes and biscuits they had brought in brown paper bags after a family party. There were moments of merriment we shared. 'I fix it for you, Liz. I fix your vacuum,' Mustafa greeted me one night after unblocking my vacuum cleaner, pointing to a straightened wire hanger hooked on an overhead pipe. If I had a problem, I could use that, he said. I must have looked mystified again. 'You put it in machine,' said Satma, sitting next to me on the broken chair. 'Oh,' I said. 'I thought Mustafa meant pull on it and he'd come running downstairs to fix it.' Satma laughed uproariously, patting my knee, which she did if she approved of something I said. But we hadn't progressed past polite gestures and probably never would. I had found another job.

Chapter 4

THE HOTELS

I HAD BEEN HIRED as a breakfast attendant by a small city hotel where I had stayed as a guest on a previous visit to Melbourne but would now work for $11.98 an hour. My first day was a Thursday in early May. There was no sign of the Melbourne winter as yet, not even at 5.35 am, when I caught the first tram along St Kilda Road, special transport for people who had to sign in by six. There were working men in watch caps fast asleep, a brown-skinned man with the carved features of an Easter Island monument and a girl with purple-streaked hair. The men I talked to another day were security guards and hospital porters. One opened up a parking station. I came to think of them as the fraternity of the first tram, but most were sunk into themselves, staring through the windows at the greystone gatehouses and playing fields of schools attended by boys and girls whose fathers didn't take the first tram to work. The one man in a suit read the *Herald Sun*, which he folded into an old briefcase before we reached Flinders Street.

The Princess Hotel was a few blocks from the tram stop. I reached the place and panicked. The door was locked. All I had been told was that my shift started at six. Five minutes to go. I thought of fleeing before anyone saw me – if there was anyone there. The night manager unlocked the door at last. He was heavy-lidded, like a monitor lizard, and didn't seem to care if I stayed or went, as long as I let him fall back in his chair and sleep. The dining room was on the next floor, he said.

I didn't know what to expect – certainly not Svetlana, as I'll call her, the one-woman reception committee who was upstairs, in a long room with cafe tables and chairs at one end and sofas at the other. A tiny, 40-something Russian immigrant with badly dyed black hair and an accent so thick you could have cut it with a knife, Svetlana announced that she was glad to see me even before we closed the distance between us and shook hands. She threw herself into the gesture and rapidly gave signs of throwing herself into everything she did, whirling between the kitchen and the dining room where a big sideboard with the top covered in frightful baize-green plastic padding had already been set with the breakfast things – plates, hot plates and toasters, jugs of juice and trays of glasses.

THE HOTELS

Svetlana and I worked together effortlessly from that day forward, though her reluctance to issue me with instructions left me bewildered at first. She had shown me over the narrow kitchen, the centre of operations, and the small room next door where the guests' room numbers and other details were entered on a touch-screen computer. I had slurped down a coffee, the first of many, and Svetlana was still repeating how happy she was to see me, as if I had rescued her from a shark-infested atoll, rather than a few days in the buffet on her own.

The woman who did the job before me had walked out. 'Don't say nothing,' Svetlana said, furiously intense, letting me know that she hadn't liked the woman, Lin, even before Lin quit in an unheard-of fashion. 'She send fax,' said Svetlana, still disbelieving. Technology intimidated her, as I saw when she gave me my first lesson on the computer, gingerly pressing the keys as if they were alive, and exclaiming in amazement when I caught on. I wondered why Lin had left inside a week. I had seldom been made more welcome or had less demanded of me. 'Is needing oranges,' she said when I coaxed her to tell me what to do – even if it was only fetching fruit from the boxes stowed under the counter.

Between 6 and 6.30, when the buffet opened for business, the bread had to be heated and the fruit sliced. The platters were arranged on the sideboard from which guests helped themselves, the same as in any other budget hotel that boasted a free continental breakfast. Only seldom required to cook and serve the hot breakfast, for which guests had to pay extra, the attendants checked room numbers, cleared tables, put the dirty dishes through the dishwasher, and refilled the platters and jugs until the buffet closed again at 10.30. Though it would take me a few days to memorise the routines and fall into the rhythm, the first day set the pattern of the job at the Princess Hotel. It was a relief to be doing a job so simple that even I could manage it — one of several pleasant surprises during my time as a breakfast attendant.

But the work wasn't what made my first day at the Princess Hotel so unforgettable. That was all Svetlana's doing. She seemed to lack any social inhibitions. I had been in my new job about ten minutes, just long enough to survey the surroundings, when Svetlana began to talk about the wretchedness of her life with her husband, Boris. I gathered that his possessiveness knew no bounds. Boris forced her to explain what she did every minute she was away from him, she said, taking the bread out of the microwave. If she came home a few minutes late, he insisted she had been meeting someone, she went on, putting the croissants in the oven, followed by the pastries. I said something, I forget what. Svetlana was still talking about Boris. I was still getting my bearings. The onslaught of information was a little overwhelming, I guess, not that I had to do anything but take it in. Svetlana had done most of what needed to be done before the guests arrived. The same thing happened every other morning we worked together.

THE HOTELS

She lived on the edge of Melbourne some 30 kilometres from the city, and caught a train at 4.30 am to get to work on time. I believe she would have caught an earlier train if she could. Because the 4.30 got to Flinders Street Station half an hour early, Svetlana reached the hotel with twenty minutes to spare, and went straight to work. Her need to be doing meant she constantly found things that had to be done that minute, from laundering the hotel curtains to removing the grease-coated vents high over the stove to clean them.

If there was a quiet moment, Svetlana leafed through the *Herald Sun* she had picked up in the lobby on her way upstairs. She had a particular radar for stories of murder and mayhem. On my first day she had already found time to discover a couple of paragraphs about a woman who tried to cut off her husband's penis because he raped her. 'Is too short,' she said. I believe she meant the story, not what remained of the penis. She had left the newspaper open at the page to show it to visitors like her friend, Rita, the breakfast attendant at the Duchess, our sister hotel.

There was frequent coming and going between the two establishments. Since the supplies were kept at the Princess, Rita would rustle in before 6.30 to pick up pastries and fruit for her kitchen 'over the other side'. A widow in her fifties with her face caked with makeup, Rita was more trillingly feminine in style than a female impersonator. She flirted with the boys on the front desk, as well as with the bow-legged man who delivered the fruit and vegetables, freshened her bright red lipstick, then returned to her domain at the Duchess.

I had been to the Duchess, where the company had its offices, for the job interview with two hotel executives. I wasn't informed of the identity of the unsmiling Japanese woman silently observing me like a lab rat from a few metres away. I didn't find out until after I was hired that her family owned the hotels. The one doing nice cop was Margot, the hotel manager, an amiable woman of about 40 who spoke with an Irish brogue. Margot said she had phoned me for an interview because she had overheard me when I filled in the application form.

I had already been to eight or nine hotels that day. I would have sworn this interview was an exercise in futility, even if the Duchess *was* less intimidating than the Grand Hyatt, where I had hidden behind a column after seeing a guy I knew checking in. In the Duchess, I was more myself, joking with the desk clerk about being the oldest person to have walked in asking for work all day. It was obvious that I liked people, Margot said, and I agreed, wondering what it had to do with making up beds. I had applied to be a room attendant, but they were hiring someone to do the breakfast shift. The other duties were mentioned only in passing.

That made the full-time job in the hotel the third one I had walked into knowing almost nothing about the job, as if one menial job was so much like the next that the people doing the hiring had decided that describing them in any detail was a waste of their time.

The Japanese woman spoke at last to say that the person they were employing would fill in as required. But if talking was a qualification for this job, I was qualified. I was hired because I can't keep quiet for long, not even while filling in a form. Bad luck if you're old and shy.

I believe that a shy person would have found Svetlana on the confronting side. But we took to each other right away. I was overjoyed that I had been thrown together with someone who badly needed to talk and did so at once, saving time. I didn't meet Boris but soon heard enough about him to give him a chapter of his own. He had left his job as a mechanic the previous year and gone on disability. He wanted to work but was frightened of losing the pension, she said, so he stayed at home all day, stewing over things, calling Svetlana's mobile phone so often the instrument could have been devised with the standard issue abusive husband in mind. He not only collected her from the train station but stood outside the bathroom door when she went in to take a bath – 'like prison', said Svetlana, her deep voice hardly more than a croak. He pocketed her earnings, giving her $100 a week.

I couldn't believe she put up with it. Though it was my first morning at the hotel, I forgot my resolutions about minding my own business and advised her to leave him. But she was frightened she would lose everything – the house they had nearly paid off, the garden with the vegetables she had grown. If she moved out, where would she go, she said, tears springing to her eyes, at almost the moment the first guest of the morning turned up.

But Svetlana's moods were as changeable as the Melbourne weather; five minutes later she was in animated conversation with a glamorous, gravel-voiced woman from Beijing who had spent all night at the casino after the boyfriend she was meeting in Melbourne stood her up. I would have liked to know why she was free to come and go from China, but Svetlana was interrogating her about the broken romance. Listening to them talk was like hearing English bend and stretch. 'You good-looking. You find someone else,' Svetlana said, so pleased by this observation she repeated it to me when the woman went upstairs.

Everyone else was just getting up. Guests arrived a few at a time until about eight o'clock, when they burst into the room as if we were giving away money instead of coffee and muffins. Suddenly it was so busy I had five chits in my hand at once, two of them 'is including' cooked breakfast, which wasn't supposed to happen. It meant that Svetlana had to stay at the stove, frying up eggs and bacon, while I raced between the buffet and the kitchen, not sure whether to ask for room numbers, clear tables, tank up the juice or cut more melon.

The rush over, we filled and refilled the dishwasher, constantly wiping down the counters so that the kitchen would look clean if anyone walked in. Svetlana, a strange mixture of childlike trust and almost paranoid suspicion, believed that someone from management was spying on her. 'That one,' she whispered, when a woman who was the dead spit of Joan Sutherland, only bigger, surged from the lifts. 'She work for Mr Tamoto . . .' Mr Tamoto was the owner. It seemed unlikely that he was delegating personal assistants to check up on the hardworking Svetlana, but one never knew. I saw La Stupenda going past again at 10.30, which is when we had to close the buffet, but never saw her again.

Soon we were visited by Margot, who breezed in, making my arrival official. The back of the kitchen was hidden behind a high partition. Margot managed to spoil the illusion of privacy by craning over it, but appeared embarrassed to catch us scoffing slivers of melon. 'You have to eat,' she said, when Svetlana nervously tried to explain. I found it difficult to relate Margot's kindness to the abject fear of management that I soon discovered riddled the organisation. On the other hand I hadn't been around the year before when five hotel employees had been sacked in one afternoon. Tamoto had learned they were going home early after signing each other out.

When we locked up the buffet and headed downstairs, another member of the family, the one who had sat in on my interview, was at the front desk, her eyes scanning the columns of figures as though she were looking through gunsights at an unsuspecting enemy. By then I knew that she was Tamoto's niece, Kimiko. If she wished to counteract the impression of friendliness Margot had given, by making it clear that the breakfast attendant was a nobody at everybody's beck and call, she should have been more than satisfied at the sight we now presented. I was lugging two large black plastic garbage bags, and tiny Svetlana was somehow hanging on to a dish of croissants, a glass bowl and a carton of supplies we were taking to the Duchess as soon as we got rid of the garbage. 'Where are you taking the croissants?' Kimiko barked at Svetlana, who seemed to have turned to stone. I put down the garbage bags a moment, vaguely thinking, 'If she doesn't know, who does?' At last, Svetlana whispered that we were taking them to the Duchess and got an earful from Kimiko, who had deduced that guests at the four-star Duchess would be getting warmed-over croissants for breakfast the following morning.

We escaped from Kimiko at last, leaving the croissants in a stairwell and heading off to the dumpster behind the hotel. The sight made my heart sink. I wished I were anywhere but in a back lane in Melbourne staring down a garbage-filled dumpster. I can't deal with some kinds of dirt. I don't know what a shrink would say, but I blame it on my mother, a woman who taught us not to be afraid of anything but who was so afraid of dirt you could have tortured her by refusing to let her wash her hands after going to the toilet. I suppressed the primal urge to run away. I didn't want to have to lift the lid when Svetlana got the lock off. I hadn't anticipated such moments when I first looked for low-wage work – moments when I confronted the necessity

THE HOTELS

of doing something I had always assiduously avoided, such as fishing a scrap of garbage from the wet grey witch-hair of a mop, which I had been forced to do that morning. I told myself I was spoiled, hesitating only an instant before lifting the dumpster lid and holding it with two fingers, risking a fracture to save on contact.

I was aching to stop and wash up, but Svetlana was off again, trotting back to the hotel to retrieve the supplies for the Duchess, before darting down the street as I followed, terrifically self-conscious in the hotel uniform. We wore a white shirt and black pants. (I had bought two shirts and the pants for $72, which would make a big dent in my first pay packet.) The hotel provided the rest of the outfit – a scarf and vest. The red vest with gilt buttons gave me a passing resemblance to a transgender bellboy. If we waited around this part of town, dotted with hotels, someone was sure to give me their luggage to carry. Fortunately, the Duchess was close by.

If I had learned anything from my limited time in the low-wage workforce it was not to ask too many questions. But not asking intrusive questions absorbed so much of my energy I was neglecting to ask the obvious ones. It was only after we reached the Duchess that morning that I picked up the pertinent information that Svetlana and I worked at two hotels, not one, going from the breakfast room of the cosy, down-at-heel Princess to the breakfast room of the Duchess, a posh little boutique hotel a five-minute walk away.

Rita had already let me know it was the best one in the chain. Like so many other smart hotels the place looked as if it had been done out by one of Philippe Starck's newest apprentices. Sometimes less is less. The ash-grey lobby was so subdued our red vests stuck out like flags at a funeral. The breakfast room upstairs was all glass and metal, the counter tops gleaming so hard you were forced to squint. It was a picture of elegance that ordinary people would have spoiled. If I had just checked in, rather than thinking about the amount of surface to clean and polish, I would have felt self-conscious venturing in for breakfast. It is one of the mysteries of our time that good hotels have replaced the country house look with one apparently inspired by the inside of a bank vault.

The Duchess continued the theme with its own surveillance system. Svetlana directed my gaze up the wall at the back and I saw why she had intimated a preference for the other hotel. There was a security camera hanging like a vulture over the kitchen at the back of the buffet. Tamoto had installed the security system after he bought the hotel.[1] Svetlana explained that we could be seen from the front desk and the office. I couldn't persuade her that management had to have better things to do than spy on three middle-aged women washing dishes and scrubbing tables, or, in my case, scrambling about trying to find the right key or the right broom closet. Nothing could shake her conviction that we were kept under surveillance.

THE HOTELS

While the Princess was full of amiable tourists on package holidays, the Duchess drew a sniffier upscale scattering of rich foreigners and executives on expense accounts. Its continental breakfast cost more than a breakfast attendant earned in one and a half hours (and the rack rate for some of its suites was more than we earned in a week). Breakfast included platters of cold meats and cheeses, which we restocked when we joined Rita over the other side, curling leftover slices of ham and pressed turkey in tasteful arrangements to tempt the punters to help themselves. Only the sprigs of parsley could be guaranteed fresh on the day. While Svetlana coaxed leftover triangles of blue vein and tiny cubes of cheddar from a smeared half-empty platter to a clean one, Rita fussed with the composition of a platter of fruit as if it was a still life and she was Cézanne. The task completed, Rita decided that a coffee break was in order, and we trooped through the side door to sit on a backstairs landing, the closest thing we had to a tearoom, though another camera hung over us there, in case we took it into our heads to steal bottles of Spray 'n' Wipe or towelling slippers from the supplies in the nearby broom cupboard.

The conversations Rita initiated often had a wistfully prurient edge. The first thing she had said to me after we were introduced was that she had five boyfriends and would give me one. When we sat on the stairs nursing strange-tasting beverages from the automatic cappuccino machine, her pride and joy, she started joking about going out with a boyfriend the night before.

The security camera forgotten, Svetlana entered into the spirit of the thing.

'Where you go with boyfriend, honey baby?'

'Take me to restaurant,' Rita replied, smiling.

Which one, Svetlana asked. Was it McDonald's? Rita had married a much older man soon after leaving the Philippines, and moved to Melbourne after his death. There was no racy social life. She went to work, then went home. Her jokes about boyfriends were like jokes about winning the lottery, but she couldn't let it go. It was an expensive restaurant, she said gaily. 'He got plenty money.'

There would soon come a day when I would rather rush off to clean toilets than hear her stories again, but I would remember my first day at the hotel for the warmth between us. Most days Rita would bring noodles or rice from home, while Svetlana would make a toasted sandwich in our kitchen (no camera!) and eat it sitting on the backstairs at the Duchess. But we celebrated my first day by going out to lunch, sitting squashed together at a table for one at a Hungry Jack's in the basement of a shopping mall a few blocks away. The place was crammed with shop assistants and office workers shouting across tables as if it was their lunch club, but my colleagues reserved Hungry Jack's for special occasions.

Rita, who headed to the counter to order the burgers and pay, refused to accept my money, four dollars something, the equivalent of about 25 minutes of her labour. The moment to pay her back passed. Rita was talking about her late husband, a kind man with such good manners he always held open the gate for her, she said. I tried to picture it. He was 60 when they met. She was 22. Yet, it was the sort of thing any woman would have remembered. I had also been married to a courtly man, a recollection I didn't share. Rita had already asked if I was married or single and I had told her I was divorced, hoping to leave it there. This was easy around Svetlana whose own obsessions wouldn't leave her alone. She was looking over her shoulder as if we were suddenly back in the old Soviet Union. Something had reminded her of the woman from Mr Tamoto's office she believed was spying on us, as she reported to Rita, making herself so nervous she consulted her watch, then mine. We had the standard half-hour lunch-break and had only been gone for quarter of an hour but, fearful of what might happen if we were five minutes late, Svetlana kept breaking into what remained of the conversation to announce the time.

Despite the evidence that it was hard to find reliable employees to turn up at six every morning for the sort of money we were earning, Svetlana seemed to feel she could be carpeted for a small mistake such as closing the buffet five minutes early or coming back five minutes late from lunch. I thought that her fear of getting sacked was out of proportion to the likelihood of it happening. Then again, her permanent job at the hotel had followed years of casual employment as a room attendant. She had supplemented her earnings as a casual by cleaning houses in Melbourne's eastern suburbs, often for as little as $10 cash an hour, which was well under the going rate. But Svetlana hadn't thought of complaining, as if she saw the 'ladies' as existing in a realm purer than her own, even as she changed their sheets and scrubbed their bathroom tiles. She had taken what work she could find – work more likely than ever to be casual, intermittent and part-time.

But Svetlana felt vulnerable on another count. For her, work was a haven from life with Boris. For Rita, it was a haven from loneliness. For both, work was the best part of their everyday lives – the last thing I would have predicted. They had a brittle friendship that my presence interrupted, but they were so isolated that Rita's only other confidante was her landlady, who lived in the same building. The woman exploited Rita's craving for respectability, charging her $180 a week, nearly half her take-home pay, for a two-bedroom flat in a northern suburb full of people with receding chins and tea-strainer vowels. I wondered what it must be like for Rita getting off the bus and going into a supermarket in which every other face was white, the faces behind the cash registers included, but she said she felt safe in the area.

Rita liked to be surrounded by the hallmarks of status, as if some of it rubbed off on the women in housekeeping. 'VIP, darling,' she said, on the afternoon of my first day there, heading off to the room of an arriving guest with a silver tray on which she had set out a bottle of wine, a wine glass, a white

THE HOTELS

napkin and, mysteriously, an apple, to convey the ineffable essence of class with which the hotel wished to be associated. Svetlana and I more prosaically vacuumed the hallways. But as I dragged the vacuum cleaner over the carpet at the Duchess, I experienced an unexpected emotion. I felt mildly euphoric. The hallway was so small compared with the office I had cleaned the night before and would clean again that evening. The euphoria didn't last.

I was now committed to two jobs – the new one at the hotel and the old one office cleaning. When the new one came up, I had made a snap decision to do both, reasoning that the $39 a night from the cleaning job would help cover living expenses like food, after I used my pay from the hotel to keep a roof over my head. What I hadn't calculated was how to fit everything in: finishing my shift at the hotel, catching a tram to St Kilda and making notes about one job before going to the other.

The hotel shift finished on the stroke of 2.30. Svetlana, martyr to the train timetable, pelted off for the 2.38, while Rita walked me to the news-stand on the nearest corner, ready to assist in the purchase of the weekly tram pass. My head thudded on to my chest seconds after I found a seat and I woke with a start somewhere along St Kilda Road, still bent over the first page of *The Age*, which I had picked up at the hotel. I had been dreaming about a distant place perched on the edge of a cliff, like my flat in Sydney, except that I was employed there as a domestic cleaner.

In my room at the Waterloo I tried to stay awake but soon gave up. I climbed between the crisp, fresh-laundered sheets, dreamily contemplating the absurdity of the situation: while I had been vacuuming at the hotel, another woman had vacuumed my room.

Next thing I knew the alarm had rung. It was almost dark – time to go to work again. Parking outside the office building, I greeted the other cleaners and went up a floor to clean the glass doors in the entrance, the first task of the evening, then dragged my trolley through the next set of doors, already wondering if I ought to give up the job. A fair-haired man still at his desk, who usually took the time to be pleasant, said things couldn't be all that bad. 'I start work at six tomorrow,' I snapped. He looked so stricken that I admitted I was masquerading as a cleaner. I gave him my name and told him about the book.

But I had worked for two weeks for people who knew me only as 'Liz'. That's what it said on the cheque Mustafa handed over when I finished work that night. The cheque was for $360 – $39 a night for ten nights with $30 taken out. 'Tax,' Mustafa said. Not my tax, though. There was no last name on the cheque. I filled it in myself and cashed it without any trouble, much to my astonishment.

It was only later that I learned the award rate for a cleaner employed as a casual in Victoria was then more than $15 an hour, which meant that beaming Bob had ripped me off to the tune of $2-something an hour, about $35 a week, nearly three hours' worth of dusting and vacuuming. I like to think of myself as hard-headed, so it's embarrassing to admit that the possibility I was being cheated out of my rightful earnings didn't cross my mind. But my lapse was instructive. Employer groups are always pressing the argument that they should be able to negotiate pay and conditions with individual employees (a situation conservative governments have done what they can to bring about), basing their case on the risible pretence that the parties come to this negotiation on an equal footing. If they were equal, the anonymous drones of the service industry would have managed to capitalise on the demand for their labour, rather than working for ten bucks an hour which is all but the industry standard in some parts of the contract cleaning industry.[2] There was that to be said in beaming Bob's defence. He was paying $3 an hour more than many contractors.

I had my money. The logical thing was to drift off into the night. But something in me resisted being typecast as the sort of person who vanished the moment she earned a few dollars. Soon after we met, Mustafa had complained about a cleaner who hadn't come back after pocketing his first pay cheque. 'I too good to people,' he'd said, as if paying a man for two weeks' work was an act of charity. Nevertheless I returned the next night for three hours of work, knowing I wouldn't be back for the money because I had decided to call it quits.

'Why you not turn out the lights?' Mustafa said when he saw me. I shoved off again with my trolley and gave the whole floor a thorough going-over, unable to dispel the idea that someone would notice how nice and clean it was before realising that the cleaner who did it had gone. 'Where's the other girl?'

There is no job more anonymous, of course. Unless they screw up and move your files around, office cleaners leave no trace behind. I couldn't help trying. It was my last opportunity to do the job properly. I was about to do something my parents would have found abhorrent – walking out on the job without giving notice. I said nothing about it to Mustafa, but I called Bob from a public phone that weekend, to say I wouldn't be back because I had found a full-time job. Feeling like the feckless sort of person who was capable of walking out like that compounded my sense of failure.

Thousands of Australians – 5 per cent of all workers and 10 per cent of workers in casual part-time positions – hold down two or more jobs to make ends meet. I had given up after exactly two days, though I was earning so little I could have been a statistic in the ACTU's annual Safety Net Review case before the Australian Industrial Relations Commission. (The workers themselves used to put in an appearance until employer groups concluded that it wasn't in their best interests to cross-examine witnesses who were sobbing as they explained why their earnings failed to cover heating bills and school shoes.)

I pocketed $395 from my full-time job that week. When Margot had called to offer me the position she said it was full-time, flexitime, four weeks' holiday a year, starting at six in the morning. She forgot to say that I would be working weekends, for the same $11.98 an hour, 63 cents an hour over what was then the federal minimum wage. No one breathed a word about penalty rates. The $27,000 Margot quoted included superannuation. The real salary was $24,918.

At half-past five on a Sunday morning in May, I found myself clomping along St Kilda Road trying not to step in dogshit or to pay attention to the creepy shadows behind the trees. I had just learned that there was no tram until about six on Sunday mornings. I would have to lash out on a taxi, spending money I could ill afford. Mumbling to myself to keep my spirits up, I trudged along in the dark for several more long blocks before I saw a vacant cab. I thought of telling the grizzled Greek cab driver my hard-luck story, but he got in first, saying he used to start work at five in the mornings, but had just been ordered to start half an hour earlier. 'It's like factory – don't come in a few times, they get someone else.' The fare nudged $10, about what I would make for an hour's work that day.

Svetlana set the pace. Despite the little we earned, I had seldom met anyone who put more heart into her work. There were moments when I wondered if she had sprung out of some era celebrated in the myths of the Employers Federation, when simple folk paid a pittance took immeasurable pride in doing simple things well. That weekend, she decided to give our domain at the Princess a thorough cleaning. The plan was confirmed with the under-manager, a stripling with Coke-bottle specs, whose name, Ernest, befitted his nature. Usually we went to the Duchess after breakfast. That morning Rita joined us instead and we spent the day in an orgy of cleaning.

Rita scratched away at stains in the chairs, telling a story about a Filipina who was to marry a guy she met after going to his house to do the ironing 'Businessman, has big house,' she said. It was her favourite fairytale ending. I was scrubbing the sideboard, bombarding the plastic padding with cleaning product. Initially reluctant to use chemicals in areas where food was served, I had started spritzing Mr Sheen and Handy Andy around like cologne. A few more days in the hospitality industry and I would be snorting the stuff when I went home.

Svetlana had bleached the cups and saucers in the dishwasher. 'Look, Liz, is clean like new,' she called out gaily, in top form, standing still for a rare moment, as if ravished by the beauty of the thick hotel crockery, before she hurled herself at the next task, and cleaned out an adjacent storeroom where the liquor was locked away. Declaring that the storeroom smelled of spilled liquor, she swabbed the shelves with vinegar, then moved her attention to the bar. Two stout German couples staying in the hotel steered past, eyes fixed on her whirling figure. They stared as if a museum exhibit had grown arms and started polishing the furniture.

The irony was that the effervescent Svetlana went home to lie in the bath for two hours, while her husband stood outside, ranting at the closed door. He had started making wild accu-

THE HOTELS

sations when he saw her talking to a man at the train station, she said. The new pattern of their home life was soon established: he said bitter and ugly things, and she refused to talk to him. 'I don't answer nothing. Don't lose words for rubbish like that,' she said, miming herself with her lips clamped shut. Everything she did was strenuous, even not speaking. We had stopped cleaning for a bit and plumped down on upturned containers or milk crates, rather than the nearby chairs and tables. Rita lunched on the rice noodles she brought from home. Svetlana and I unwrapped the cheese and salami sandwiches she had made at 11.30, toasting the bread which was kept in the freezer. The toast was stone cold by the time we ate it. Since we were sitting near the sideboard where the toaster had been put away, rather than in the stairwell of the other hotel, my hand itched to reach for it, but Svetlana was sure that someone from management would know we were bending the rules, and pounce, catching us redhanded with two bits of bread and a toaster. But the only employee nearby was the middle-aged man who did the vacuuming at the Princess (while we did the vacuuming in the other hotel, a division of labour that I liked to imagine enshrined in an enterprise agreement).

When George ploughed past with his vacuum cleaner, Rita took it into her head to tease him. 'When you taking us out, George? You a lucky man. Three ladies to go out with you.' 'I'll take the three of you out to a restaurant,' he said. 'You have a restaurant, George?' asked Rita and he replied that he didn't *own* a restaurant but would take us out anyway. George was quiet and self-effacing. Unless management was prowling around, I would offer him a coffee and a muffin. Control of a supply of caffeine was a perquisite of my new position. I could trade it for information – or, in George's case, for taking the garbage out to the dreaded dumpster. He had stopped by the day before and said that management had asked him to stay on for four more hours. That meant a twelve-hour day at everybody's beck and call, carting furniture and luggage all over the hotel. I asked if he minded, but he said he didn't – he was glad of the extra hours. His rent had just been put up $100 a month and he wasn't sure if he could manage.

Others managed by paring down all other expenses. Rita's flat was the one luxury she permitted herself. Svetlana and Boris had bought their quarter-acre piece of the Australian dream years before, and had nearly paid it off. They didn't go out at night or away on holidays, even when Boris had worked. They had no children. They lived simply. What money they made went into the mortgage and on several of those entertainment devices the top dogs from the chamber of commerce so begrudged working people. The sound system had thus far survived Boris's habit of breaking things in the house when he flew into a rage. Though they lived in a state of siege, they still scrimped and saved as if building a future together. Boris was on a pension and Svetlana on minimum wages, but they had put a deposit on a small flat – an investment property! – a few streets from where they lived. How they had managed to purchase it I had no idea.

It wasn't the sort of mystery I had expected to come across when I started my project, any more than I had anticipated meeting the likes of Svetlana, who needed to work to escape from home. But the pleasure she took in her work was so real I briefly shared it, glancing with satisfaction at the results of our labours as if there was satisfaction to be had.

Most days we finished the breakfast shift at the Princess and hightailed it to the Duchess to join Rita for the part of the job that defied job description. The company employed the three of us for eight hours a day to cover the breakfast shift. Making it a full-time permanent position gave the breakfast attendants added incentive to keep turning up at 6 am (one reason I had concluded that Svetlana's fears of being fired were needless). What we did for the last few hours of the working day didn't seem to matter, as long as we kept ourselves busy, polishing door handles, picking leaves and stray cigarette butts out of the planter boxes on the roof garden, and cleaning 'public areas' – that is, toilets. Had I stopped to think about it before joining the low-wage workforce, I would have assumed that cleaning public toilets was a trial one had to train for, abasing oneself by degrees. Cleaning toilets was one of life's positional markers. The concept of class may have been consigned to the dustbin of history (as if wealth and poverty were equal starting positions), but one thing was certain: people who cleaned other people's lavatories belonged in a different class from people who never cleaned their own. I nerved myself up to it, then found that I didn't mind swishing Domestos around the public areas.

There were other small indignities that bothered me more, such as collecting wet bathrobes from hotel rooms and stuffing them into laundry bags with my bare hands. I stifled actual physical revulsion as I grabbed robes that were wet or muddy, as if people wiped their shoes on them, which they wouldn't think of doing at home.

Entering the rooms that showed signs of human occupation made me uncomfortable, in any case. I had imagined that going into hotel rooms with open suitcases and possessions scattered about would give me glimpses of life in the raw. Instead, I rushed in and out of the rooms with eyes only for the contents of the mini-bar. That was one of the few tasks Margot had mentioned when she interviewed me for the position – breakfast from six, then stock rotation and mini-bars. Still in our fetching uniforms, of course, Svetlana and I wandered through the five floors of the hotel clowning around a little as we knocked on doors and called out 'Housekeeping' or 'Mini-bar'. Under Svetlana's tutoring I soon learned to spot at a glance if miniature bottles of Jim Beam were missing from the mini-bar. Under Rita's tutoring I learned to construct pyramids of perfectly rolled towels, furnishing the hotel gym, a place where I, too, liked to retreat on my own to work off tensions – not by climbing on the exercise machines, of course, but by dusting them.

THE HOTELS

Sometimes I got down on my hands and knees to scrub the tiled floor outside the steamroom, marvelling at finding myself in this abject position, especially when a 30-something hotel guest, whose suitcase I had just carried to her room, tripped across the tiles in her high heels and looked in, saying she was thinking of using the steamroom after work. I didn't need a steamroom – I was red-faced and sweating. In truth, I felt a bit smug, like an ascetic doing some serious penance, though I was just on my hands and knees (as some workers are every day of their lives), my bum pointed in the general direction of the security camera.

There was no rational explanation for the rush to get from one hotel to the other: from almost the moment we reached the Duchess until 2.30 knock-off time, we were busy with an elaborate make-work program. We ran towels over spotless exercise machines and flicked virtual dust from fixtures dusted the day before, if not that morning. What little research I had done before stumbling into a job in a hotel had led me to believe I would meet employees under pressure from managements that had redefined the demands of the job until nine or ten hours of monotonous work were crammed into eight. I had been interviewed for a job at one big Sydney hotel with a workplace agreement that said room attendants had to make up thirteen rooms a shift – an endurance trial typical of the demands on many hotel employees.

The room attendants at the Tamoto hotels were casuals working for a company that paid them by the hour. (According to Jane Farrell, assistant state secretary of the Victorian branch of the Liquor, Hospitality and Miscellaneous Workers Union, enterprise agreements are rare, and there is no mention of room quotas in the award, but organisers from the union are uncovering cases involving some smaller contract companies that ordered room attendants to make up 24 rooms in a seven-hour shift – finishing each day's quota in their own time.) Those I met, over the bundles of dirty linen piled up in the hallways, were young women from the Sudan and Ethiopia. It was as though even in multicultural Melbourne there were unspoken rules about race that harked back thousands of years: the darker the skin, the heavier the load. Rita and Svetlana frequently criticised their standards as room attendants, as if there was a contest on. But the young women were making up the rooms, the job only the strong survived, while we passed a pleasant half-hour checking that each room had its quota of slippers and robes.

If I had expected to be buckling under the workload, my timing was wrong again. The budget hotels in the chain were busy all year round, but the lull had hit the Duchess, abandoned like the wreck of the *Hesperus*, though my shipmates and I were still there, running hand towels along skirting boards and over light fixtures. But during the slow period in winter they could give their bodies a rest, Rita said, as we gave the elevator doors an extra polish. In the busy season, they might be expected to work seven, eight or nine days in a row, leaping in as room attendants as required.

THE HOTELS

This was set out in the contract Margot produced one morning, during my second week at the hotel, striding into the kitchen of the Princess and craning over the partition to ask how I was settling in. The note of concern wasn't reflected in the contract, which explained the concept of flexi-hours at considerable length. The nub of it was that the company had complete call on my time 24/7 and could demand more or less than 40 hours a week without advance notice or consultation 'where business circumstances or unexpected absences or demands for labour create a need to alter the roster'.

Naturally the flexibility was all on one side. Though we were forced to invent tasks straight out of *Gosford Park*, cleaning back stairs doors or polishing door handles to kill the unending half-hour from 2 to 2.30, with sneak-cam doing its job, there was no question of lounging around and no hope of going home early if we had finished our work for the day. Svetlana said that a lot of people used to go home early, but not any longer. Mr Tamoto had wandered into the Princess one afternoon and failed to find anyone. That was the day he sacked five employees at once, striking fear into the hearts of all who were still employed. But the day I met my elderly white-haired boss, he was as polite as he was distracted. The hotel was in an uproar, as I heard after an absence of two days.

Tuesdays and Wednesdays were my days off and I savoured them to the full. I dozed through the rumble of the linesmen's trucks which left the Waterloo at six, and did my laps with the idle rich at the gloriously named Harold Holt Memorial Pool in suburban Malvern, then splurged on breakfast at a cafe in a part of Prahran more comfortably fixed in time than a person from Sydney had any right to expect. I had been out to breakfast both days, spending $18 I should have kept to buy provisions. Svetlana had given me such a startled look when I said I liked to go out for breakfast on my day off that I never mentioned it again.

When Thursday dawned, it was pouring with rain. The fraternity of the first tram was silent all the way into the city, staring through the steamed-up windows at the black ribbon of the river. One of the regulars was missing. He had said his goodbyes the previous week after travelling into the city for years and years, seeing the same faces, on the way to the hospital where he worked as an orderly. He had always greeted everyone at his end of the tram – he seemed to be that sort of man – but he usually sat with a security guard who was most unlike him. I thought of the security guard as the Bitter Celt, because his last positive memory seemed to be of the Battle of the Boyne. He had pronounced opinions on everything, even at 5.35 am. Without the other man there, no one said anything, least of all the Bitter Celt, who seemed lost.

But Svetlana, in the buffet bright and early as usual, was busting to tell me something. She was triumphant. 'You won't believe what is happening,' she called out, her face alight with laughter. An inspector was coming that day to poke around to check if the Princess still justified its three-star rating. The day before, the management had looked in vain for half a dozen sufficiently clean rooms to show the dreaded inspector.

'You won't believe. Eight rooms. Not one cup, not one glass is clean,' said Svetlana, who had stayed back to help Tamoto, his niece and their managers fix up the rooms. They kept whisking in and out that morning during the nerve-racking wait for the inspector to arrive. 'You must be Liz,' Mr Tamoto said, shaking me by the hand. Hours later, towards the end of the inspector's visit, I saw him with Kimiko, huddling in a doorway at the mouth of the lane opposite the hotel, waiting for the verdict. The inspector gave the hotel its stars without so much as a peek in our kitchen, but the two of them were still in the doorway fifteen minutes later when Svetlana and I passed by. I couldn't help feeling sorry for them, though we were the ones schlepping the garbage and they were the ones with the right to go through our belongings to see if we had stolen anything.

Svetlana had warned me that our bags might be checked when we finished work for the day, but nothing of the sort happened during my time at the hotel. I never knew which fears sprang from her feverish imagination and which ones were justified. But other employees there were no less fearful. The front desk clerks whispered Mr Tamoto's name as if it could explode in their faces. I would leave the job without seeing a demonstration of the power that frightened them so.

Even allowing for the cameras, management seemed low-key to me. I didn't hear Margot address subordinates with anything but respect, so unusual an approach in my experience of the low-wage workforce that I concluded she was experimenting with some strange new management technique that suggested allowing workers some dignity. And from my perspective, it worked. In the first few weeks in the job, I almost imagined that I could go on indefinitely, falling into a pattern whereby my body adjusted to rising at five o'clock, even in the dead of winter, to see what surprises awaited me in the buffet.

The Princess did packages of less than $100 a night (for a room so small you could unpack while lying in bed). The three-star package included our five-star smiles. Our omelettes were nothing to write home about, but there could hardly have been two breakfast attendants in all Melbourne who were less jaded, or more likely to linger to talk to people for the pleasure of it. I took my cues from Svetlana, who relished that part of the job and gave me lessons in hospitality without even knowing it, extending the concept of service by bending the rules a little if people came in early or late for breakfast, one of our prerogatives when no one from management was about. At six in the morning, for instance.

I arrived one morning to find Svetlana talking with three crestfallen young men from Singapore who had spent the night at the casino, lost their money and come back with long faces. 'Is been to casino again,' she told me, as they forgot their troubles long enough to devour the pastries she had set out for them, turning the functional breakfast room of the Princess into something special.

Later that morning I saw her staring up at the television set we were supposed to leave on with an expression of withering contempt. The Russian-language program she had turned to was showing a military parade somewhere in the Ukraine. 'Look,' she said savagely. 'They got no food, but they march. Stupid.' The camera had moved in on an old soldier with a chestful of medals. 'Drop in water, 'e sink,' she declared, as the guests at the nearest table looked up worriedly. They were modest older people from a town near the Victorian border who stacked their plates when they were finished eating and apologised if they left anything, even a tiny container of jam. People they knew probably just watched television, rather than living along with it. But before they went home they stopped by to thank us, saying we had helped to make their stay in Melbourne enjoyable.

The immediate monetary rewards were less gratifying, of course. In my first two weeks at the hotel the $395 in my pay packet left $115 for other expenses after I had paid for my motel room. I should have found a room more in line with my income, but I was seized by inertia once I moved in. A place more in line with my income would have had the bathroom down the hall. Compared with that, I lived in the lap of luxury. Outside my window at the motel I could see a sliver of sky, the top of a pine tree, and a pair of pigeons who had taken up residence on the roof next door. The world of St Kilda forcefully intruded only on Saturday nights when drunken kids tottered along the street, and ambulance and police sirens fractured what remained of the quiet. Now and then a hooker got in, sneaking up the firestairs through the laundry if one of her tricks had tricked Brian by renting a room for the night. But that was rare. The rest of the time, the Waterloo was as respectable as a church hall. I couldn't imagine finding a cheaper place close to a tram stop that gave me the same safe feeling about leaving my laptop lying around. I dreaded the prospect of moving, in fact, having settled in. Apart from the breakfasts on my days off, I couldn't see where else to cut costs.

Most days I swam after work at the City Baths, in a magnificent old building a few tram stops from the hotel. That was $5, while the Malvern pool was $4.50, which meant that doing my laps set me back $29 a week. The weekly tram ticket was $22.50, the taxi to work on Sundays was another $10, and after all the weeks in Melbourne I was confronted with an additional expense I had forgotten to factor in – $19.60 for a month's supply of hormone replacement therapy. I had also copped a parking fine on the Sunday I had driven into the city to save the cabfare – and parked on the block Ernest had earnestly recommended, saying that no one got booked there on Sundays. We were forgetting that a car with interstate plates was pure bait for a parking cop. I cheated and paid the fine on my credit card. There was next to nothing left over for food,

THE HOTELS

let alone for emergencies, but throwing caution to the wind, I ate anyway: using a plate as a cutting board and a nailbrush to wash the dishes, I cooked potatoes and carrots in the microwave or dined on biscuits and cheese. Because most vegetables congealed into a lump of ice in the motel fridge, it was like revisiting salad-deprived Ireland right there in my motel: the only green in my diet one week was a scrap of lettuce from Svetlana's beloved garden.

But my income in those weeks was princely compared to what I pocketed without the benefit of the tax-free threshold. Margot took some convincing that I wasn't eligible, but I insisted. When my details were adjusted, at last, I suddenly seemed to be paying more tax than Kerry Packer. With $194 taken out in tax, my take-home pay plunged to $285.45, which meant I was earning $57.09 a day, or about $7.14 an hour. I could live on it only if I swapped my motel room for a bunk at the backpacker hostel, then $24 a night. Instead of economising, I did the opposite, giving up any attempt to live on my earnings, a hopeless quest by then. I went on swimming for the sake of my health, which I couldn't have permitted myself if the whole thing was for real, and I lashed out on takeaway salads because my skin had broken out for the first time in years. I threw more money around, buying a $26 fleece vest in a Target sale to wear under the one winter jacket I had brought with me. It was three degrees in the outer suburbs on the coldest mornings, but my winter clothes were in my closet at home. I hadn't expected to be in Melbourne so long. Two weeks into the job, I was counting the days.

Since washing dishes and talking to guests were the only real requirements of the position, it was one job for which I demonstrated a degree of competence (even flair, if you counted the talking). On one of Svetlana's days off I almost managed on my own, though it has to be said that I was so startled when a big table suddenly ordered 'the cooked' that I forgot to say 'the chef is sick', as instructed by Svetlana, and rushed in and out of the kitchen radiating such frazzle that I was cheered on by the guests, who seemed to have entered into the spirit of the thing.

But trouble had loomed in the most unexpected form. I could put up with the work but not the workers. I had no patience with Rita. I tried to remind myself of her kindness the first day we worked together, but the memory was wearing thin. Rita carped about Svetlana the moment her friend's back was turned. They confided in each other because each understood the other's helplessness in the face of people stronger than themselves, but Rita was constantly levering for advantage. When we worked together one day because Svetlana had to take Boris to hospital, Rita contrived to ask about the soy milk in the fridge. I had kept some back to use in my coffee, I said carelessly, and Rita immediately rang downstairs to ask if we were allowed to order extra soy milk for the staff. She must have known the answer would be no. I thought that was the end of the trouble she could make over a litre of soy milk, but

I was wrong. Rita and Svetlana usually phoned each other after a day off, dramatising all that had happened in the course of the day. That evening was no exception.

By the time I reached the hotel the next morning, Svetlana had consulted with Ernest and was in a right state, anxiously telling me that we had to be careful, management was watching us. With 72 guests there wasn't a moment to spare, but when we had closed up our side, locking the refrigerator and the bar, the door to the kitchen and the sideboard outside (to stop any unscrupulous thief swiping the tiny pods of jam and marg), I marched to the other side with the usual armful of supplies, spotted Ernest at the front desk and started bellowing at him from across the lobby that I couldn't believe all the fuss about a fucking litre of soy milk, quote unquote. It wasn't the image of itself a hotel likes to present: a lackey dressed like a plump and elderly bellboy shouting obscenities in the lobby. Pierre, the next one up the management chain, rapidly stepped in to remind me where I was. Lowering my voice, I accused Ernest of upsetting Svetlana. I didn't know that she had been so anxious, *she* had approached *him*. Imagining that I was protecting a vulnerable co-worker, I had leaped in without knowing all the facts. Affronted by the pettiness of it, I furiously whispered that a culture of fear operated at the hotel. I didn't hear any more about it from management, but I dare say my outburst helped to hobble their disappointment when I worked up the nerve to quit.

I had worried about it for days. What would I say? When would I say it? When I had informed the manager at the Club that I was leaving, the speed with which I was hustled out blurred my finer feelings. The hotel was different. I felt more obligated. But my guilt at leaving them in the lurch was complicated by the realisation that my conscience would force me to stay on another week and a bit to see them through the long weekend.

'How is your mother?' Svetlana tentatively asked one morning soon after, giving me the opening I needed. Convenient old mum. She wasn't well, I said. I would probably have to go back to Sydney to look after her. 'Ah no, don't tell me that,' she said. 'Every time I like someone, they go away.' Margot was nice to the end. 'Family comes first,' she said, when I quit.

Over at the Duchess, I found stacks of towels in storerooms and carted them up to the gym, accustomed to creating my own make-work program by then, but my ingenuity failed me towards the end of the shift, and I trailed into the guest laundry where Rita and Svetlana were rubbing virtual spots off the washing machines as they stood gossiping about people they had worked with as room attendants. They were getting their slightly tattered friendship back on track. I had interrupted it for a while but would soon be gone.

'Oh Liz, take me with you,' Svetlana called out on the last morning we worked together. The counsellor she had consulted that week could offer a bed in a shelter, nothing more. Hiding

THE HOTELS

from Boris would mean leaving the job behind. But there was no one else to count on and nowhere else to go. Her parents were dead. Her one sibling was still in Russia. 'Take me with you,' she said again, tearful as we wished each other goodbye. 'We work together – clean houses for people. We work good together.'

She had her day off on my last day. Management sent one of the desk clerks upstairs to help with the washing up. I was leaving just when I could almost manage on my own. Rita and I blew air-kisses and that was that. At the front desk, Ernest tossed the 'Liz' badge into a box full of badges and the scarf and vest into a bag for laundry, and I wandered away forever and caught the tram. The afternoon light burnished the leaves which were falling steadily as rain. I regretted not walking through the Botanic Gardens one last time, but I couldn't get away fast enough. I was on the highway heading back to Sydney by six o'clock the next morning. Svetlana had left a message. I called back before I reached the Victorian border and she repeated what she had said over and over the last time I saw her. 'Liz, take me with you.' I kept hearing the words, like a ghostly echo, as I crossed into New South Wales again.

Chapter 5

THE STORE

I TOOK TWO DAYS to drive home, stopping over in Gundagai, which I had last visited at the age of twelve when my family drove to Melbourne in the holidays and we stayed overnight. Still a bit delirious from drinking in country life after our car and caravan were surrounded by the mob of sheep Dad had stopped for out on the road, waving to the stockman like he knew him, we fell in love at first sight with Gundagai and camped near the Murrumbidgee, breathing the fresh muddy smell only rivers have. It was a mistake to go there again. The dog on the tuckerbox wasn't where I remembered it, and the motel owner glared at me as if I reminded him of his ex-wife.

There was more to smile at in Yass, which was an hour closer to home. I checked my mobile, standing on a street corner in the whistling wind, and picked up a message from a Sydney store where I had dropped off an application form three months earlier. It was one of any number of forms I had scattered about. Hearing from the company as I was on my way back to Sydney, two days after my last shift at the hotel, was so serendipitous a coincidence that I knew I would get the job and everything would be jake. I was half right.

The Store was in a big shopping mall in a suburb I'll call Middleton. The quaint ivy-covered cottages in the neighbourhood changed hands for more than a million, not that $1 million is much to write home about in Sydney these days, but the glittering, overlit mall, with its mall smell of confectionery and floral bouquets, could have been almost anywhere. Almost. In the days before the old definitions of class were scrapped, you would have called Middleton upper–middle class. The mall had a domed roof and five dizzying floors of shops. There were glass-bottomed elevators, so you could read off brand names – LauraAshleyTandyDarrellLeaDavidJones, the only ordinates in a mall – vertically as well as horizontally.

The Store occupied the basement. Racks of tracksuit pants and zip-up fleece jackets stretched as far as the eye could see. The racks of women's clothing led to racks of men's clothing which looked much the same, only bigger, as if the Chinese, who manufactured the stuff, were secretly turning us into a nation of gender benders without anyone noticing. What I noticed instead was an excess of frilly underthings in fabrics no one in their right mind would wear next to their skin. The office was past Lingerie. I had to thread my way through racks of bras and camisoles, like an obstacle course dreamed up by a pervert, to get to the meeting room where the interview was held. Carla, from human resources, had set it up for the end of the same week I finished my last shift at the hotel, which added to my complacent sense that everything was running to plan.

'Carla's in a meeting,' said the stocky, fair-haired man who met me instead. Martin gave me the wrong impression of my future workplace by being personable, pointing out, after studying my résumé, that we had grown up in the same part of Sydney. I nearly had a heart attack when he said he remembered Paris Frocks, where I had claimed to have worked for two years. It certainly gave me my start in retail. I was hanging up dresses there at the age of twelve, which is how old I was when my mother opened Paris Frocks. Luckily, Martin had moved on. But his attempt to set me at ease had had the opposite effect, making me so wary I kept imagining he was trying to catch me out. He asked what suggestions I had made to improve things at work. The résumé in front of him suggested that the options were limited. I had left the one that said I had been a housewife for eighteen years, then worked casually as a cleaner and function waiter. I don't remember my reply.

Martin then asked what I would bring to the Store. The

question came straight off the list in front of him, as far as I could tell, but was so strangely phrased that it took me a moment too long to realise that he was asking what I could contribute to the organisation. Frightened of giving myself away, I neglected to say the obvious – energy, hard work, willingness, a positive attitude, all in the space of three weeks – and said I was quick on the uptake. He made a note. I guess it was the wrong answer.

The company had over 100 stores, and employed more than 100,000 people around the country, about half of them casuals, judging by industry figures.[1] With those sorts of numbers, the interview may have been no more than a formality to screen out the visibly disturbed and chronically incapable. But did that mean Martin wanted standard answers to his standard questions? The whole thing was surreal.

What was I proud of, he asked. I waited a beat too long again before relating part of an incident that had occurred in the breakfast room of the Princess Hotel. A woman had collapsed and I had dealt with it coolly and efficiently, I said. In fact, all I had done as other guests loosened her clothes and fanned her was to call the front desk and spend some time convincing Ernest to phone for an ambulance. If you're about to collapse in a hotel, as I learned that day, the sensible course is to warn hotel staff beforehand of your room number.

Martin consulted his list again. What were my regrets? I said something about not having a proper career. I could see that poor Martin didn't know if he should give me a job or not. I hoped it wasn't because I had failed the personality test. The only other one I had come across was Pizza Hut's attempt to see if I was enough of a 'team player' to dob in fellow employees, but proponents of the tests claimed that practically all the best firms used them.[2] There might be a second interview, he said. I didn't hear anything, so I called after a week. 'Carla will phone you tomorrow,' Martin told me. Carla didn't call. I called her instead. If you're on the wrong side of 40 and the résumé you've produced is thinner than the paper it's printed on, take it from me, you're better off making a pest of yourself. In my limited experience, employers of low-wage labour still follow the course of least resistance. 'Can I phone you on Monday?' said Carla. She didn't call. I waited until Tuesday to contact her. Ten minutes ticked past before she picked up the phone and spoke with great rapidity. 'We can offer you a casual position.' I had joined the throng. This was a far more typical offer of work than the offer from the hotel.

Casual jobs accounted for two-thirds of the increase in total employment since 1990.[3] Large numbers were in retail. The Australian Council of Trade Unions had just published a paper called 'The Future of Work' which reported that there were 550,000 casuals in the retail trade. 550,001. 'Can you start tomorrow?' Carla asked. It was two in the afternoon. What if I had called her the day after? What if I hadn't called at all? Not that Carla was talking about what we used to think of as a *job*.

'You may be asked to work any hours from nought to 38 a week, did Martin tell you?'

I cancelled an appointment with the periodontist, wondering if Carla gave new employees who had children or frail parents to care for time to make other arrangements before starting three days of training. Like me, they probably wouldn't have dared to ask, in case the casual position was snatched away again, because the whole process of applying for a job – even a job from nought to 38 hours a week – was calculated to make you feel like a supplicant, grateful for any scraps of work on offer.

It had rained all night. I dressed in my Melbourne uniform (further amortising the cost of the white shirts and black trousers I had bought to wear in the hotel), with a sober black jacket instead of the gilt-buttoned vest, which reminded me how pleased I was to be back in my apartment with everything I owned at my disposal. Middleton was a 40-minute drive through parts of Sydney where a person getting a few shifts a week in retail couldn't afford to live – unless they were the people to whom Reg Hamilton, industrial advocate for the Australian Chamber of Commerce and Industry, referred when he said that Australian Bureau of Statistics household statistics showing a widening income gap failed to take into account that 'many low-income people lived in very wealthy families'.[4]

I found a parking spot a long way off and splashed through puddles to the mall, charging past the rows of undies and into the office on the dot of 9.30 to meet Sam the trainer. Sam looked about twenty years old and had curly black hair over a face as blank and pale as a piece of paper. He conspicuously consulted his watch to let me know I was in the nick of time, before explaining that the training session would be shorter than usual because there were only two trainees. He said we would do the rest of the induction with a larger group of trainees the following week, and seated himself at one end of the long table in the training room. I sat at the other end and got the ghost of a grin from the other trainee, a fair-haired, slightly doughy-looking Irishwoman in her thirties. The collar of her white shirt was frayed and her dark jacket and trousers had seen better days. Mary exuded a faint air of desperation. Her family was in Ireland and she was alone in Sydney, for reasons she didn't explain when we went to lunch together later in the day. She had followed me to the far end of the training table and we kept our heads down, industriously filling in a stack of forms. There were tax file forms and contact details, birthdates and addresses, all in triplicate. The last thing we had to sign was a declaration promising not to pilfer from the Store. I thought of asking why executives believed that signing a piece of paper would have a deterrent effect on the criminal mind. But there was no one to ask. Sam had collected the forms, switched on a video and buggered off, saying we could find him in the pay office if it ended before he came back.

I took advantage of his absence to take notes. The fact that I put pen to paper provoked Mary to do the same, so we both sat there scribbling. The first of the four videos was the company's mission statement, a piece of advertising that would never have passed an advertising standards test, though I could verify one of its claims. 'The moment the customer walks in the door they're surprised.' Shocked was more like it. I had walked through the place several times by then. It always had the tempest-tossed look of a store deluged by customers on the first day of the annual sale, with piles of clothes on the floor and heaps of shoes scattered about the Shoe Department, broken chairs in Furniture, and packets of sheets with the wrapping torn in Manchester. Only there was no sale. It had crossed my mind that the whole effect was calculated to convince shoppers they really were getting bargains galore. I could think of no other explanation for the tawdriness.

Something else was bothering me as I watched the video, even if I was being paid for doing so. Since they were hiring part-time casuals by the truckload, the procedures presumably had to be as standardised as the production of navy tracksuit pants at the company's couturier houses in China. But the mission statement was like the ballyhoo from US corporations. The voice-over had just made the risible claim that 'a shopping environment second to none helps them select merchandise easily and quickly. But sometimes customers do need our help . . . make eye contact with a customer and greet them in a natural cheerful way'. That sort of tripe used to provoke guffaws of derision from Australians. We had to be losing our scepticism if bullshit from the marketing people insinuating themselves into every process was being passed off as part of the training.

A union official had told me beforehand that there were thousands of part-time employees the company gave a shift or two a week so that they were on the books for the Christmas spree. The video claimed that the company gave casuals 'continuous training'. 'I know someone who started off as a casual and eventually became a manager,' said an employee dressed in the standard white shirt and dark trousers, chirpier than anyone I would meet in my short, unhappy career with the Store.

There was the inevitable video about harassment packed with cant from the relevant legislation, and a video about manual handling that demonstrated how to lift heavy parcels without hurting your back. When the picture show was over, Sam took us on a tour of stockrooms, emergency exits and firedoors. I had wandered right around the Store when I dropped off the application form, but the training didn't include a tour of the different departments, and I worked there on and off for five weeks without confirming how one crossed over from Electronics to Lighting, or where they had hidden the rest of the gardening equipment the Store was phasing out – information I would have imagined as more vital to the future of the vast enterprise than a quarter-hour of puff from marketing.

Somewhere between the stockroom and the evacuation point, we met Siham, a dark-eyed, worn-looking woman introduced as our supervisor. Sam informed her that we had just started three days of training, but Siham had only one question: were we working on Sunday? I said no – Sunday was my birthday. Without another word to me, Siham turned to Mary, who quickly volunteered to work that day. She needed the money, Mary said, when Sam told us to take half an hour for lunch and we went upstairs.

While the newest shopping malls incorporated community centres and libraries, as if these scant public amenities could only be justified if a property developer was involved, the ample amenities in Middleton were scattered from one end of the suburb to the other. But the mall seemed to be the centre of suburban life just the same, drawing equal numbers of solitary senior citizens and escaping mothers to the food court, where we had plunked ourselves down at a table outside a sandwich shop. I offered to shout Mary lunch. She didn't mind admitting that money was tight, but declined the offer of a toasted foccacia. Buying herself the fish and chips deal for $6, she fell on it hungrily. I insisted on buying our coffees but it made her uncomfortable, as if it committed her to something she felt she could ill-afford, such as friendship with a fellow employee. In Sydney a little under a year, she said she had always gone from one office job to the next – until she lost the last one. I had the impression that there must be more to it. Mary's shirt was a greyish-white and her shoes needed heeling. Though she looked as if she had run out of money a long time ago and was only just keeping up appearances, she steadfastly refused to accept a little loan to tide her over until payday. Long before that day she had vanished without warning, accentuating my sense of working at the Store in isolation, even if I was on checkout, in arm's reach of a fellow employee, with a queue of customers stretching all the way back to the first racks of sloppy joes.

Martin and Carla had told me in advance that there might be no work some weeks, but I was less worried about this job than I had been about the others. Because I had worked in shops as a kid and my mother had worked in shops all her life, I thought of retail as in my blood. I would soon learn differently.

Linda, a middle-aged supervisor with a red nose and a cold, handed Mary and me the training manual for checkout staff, put 'Staff training in progress' signs at adjoining checkouts and left us puzzling over it. The English was coagulated and the instructions were out of date. How checkout staff born and raised in the Philippines or Uruguay or Lebanon were expected to struggle through it was a mystery. The instructions didn't match the equipment in front of us or the cash registers in the rest of the Store. When I approached Linda after two hours and said we would pick it up more readily by standing next to a checkout person, she said we first had to read the manual – more than 100 pages of theory about voids and refunds, cheques and credit cards.

I practised operations on the cash register until it seized up, then leafed through the rest of the manual until it was time to go. The manual was seven years old, the prices were out of date, there were no store coupons or credit card forms to use when the training exercise called for them, and my cash register had stopped working altogether. Despite the comfortable shoes which had got me through thus far, my feet ached from standing in the one place all afternoon and I had the impression I would be stuck on checkout and stand still some more.

I had started off the job that day knowing only what I had heard from some union people – that they found the company more difficult to deal with than other big retailers. The video about harassment shown as part of our training had said the company recognised that employees were 'entitled to a workplace . . . in which they are treated with courtesy, dignity and respect', but I finished the day with a sense of foreboding that my first encounter with a fellow employee the next morning did little to dispel.

I brushed past Lingerie into the staff area and rather tentatively asked the big blonde in the manager's office if she could open the pay office so I could leave my handbag there for the day. Sam had suggested that Mary and I leave our things in the office until we were given keys to lockers of our own, but this explanation had no effect on Big Blonde. 'Tough shit if there's no one here when you want to get it out,' she said. Welcome to the Store!

THE STORE

We had been instructed to come in for three full days of training, but the second day's training made me almost nostalgic for the first. To start with I was teamed with a heavily made-up 40-something Indonesian called Kuma, who prompted me by stating the bleeding obvious — 'Give t'ree dollars back'... 'Take five dollar note' — but couldn't slow herself down long enough to explain what she did if a customer handed her money for an electricity bill, along with the goods. My theory about learning from the other cash register operators may have been optimistic. When I took Kuma's place at the register, she would reach around me to press keys rather than waiting for me to work it out for myself.

This part of my training was suddenly interrupted mid-morning when the supervisor asked me to stand in the store entrance to relieve an employee going on her break. Christine, a stolid, heavyset woman of about my age, who was one of a fast-dwindling number of permanent employees, usually worked in security, which meant standing in the entrance looking into customers' shopping bags to see if they had pinched anything. Christine had just one piece of advice: be careful not to touch the customers or their bags. I already knew what not to do if someone came down the escalator or stepped from the lift brandishing a gun. The bit about break-ins in one of the videos shown the previous day advised us not to try to be a hero. But I wouldn't have minded one or two more tips before going into the security business for the first time. Some genius in head office had come up with a campaign reminding staff that shoplifting cut into company profits (well, duh) by plastering notices about it all over the staffroom, but from where I stood in the firing line, the campaign was so much hot air.

Christine had instructed me to check the shopping bags of the customers who walked out past me rather than going through the checkout. I dutifully peered into the Grace Bros and David Jones bags they held open. Since the tour the previous day hadn't included so much as a peek at the stock, I didn't have the faintest idea if the bags contained pilfered goods from the Store. I reported as much to the supervisor, red-nosed Linda, who gave me a helpless look. I went back to my station, fending off questions about the whereabouts of slippers and blenders, hammers and vases, saying 'Sorry, I don't know – I'm new' so often I felt I should get a form printed. Marketing could attend to it. Instead, Linda presented me with a badge that said 'In training' and asked if I could work on Saturday from 11.30 until 2.30. I said I had a long drive for so short a shift, and she pointed out that all shifts were for three or four hours, a detail that had eluded me until that moment.

The retail agreement I later laid my hands on said that casual employees were to be employed for a minimum of three hours a shift, except in Western Australia, South Australia and Tasmania, where they could be employed for as little as two hours a stretch, which probably meant that some had to spend up to three-quarters of an hour on the road for each hour they were paid, because they couldn't find work closer to home.

THE STORE

My first stint in security over, I was sent back to stand next to Kuma. She said that she didn't mind the three-hour shifts, then lapsed into silence again. Kuma practised a still stricter economy in her exchanges with customers. If things scanned without a hitch, she rang them up wordlessly before barking 'Cashout?' The question brought gap-toothed smiles to the faces of two women dressed in layers of colourful clothes, as if they had stepped straight out of some village in the Andes into the Middleton mall to dump armfuls of clothes on the counter in front of Kuma. They took the maximum, $300 each, their faces still wreathed in smiles as I folded their purchases into the Store's shopping bags, thinking about the 19 or 20 per cent interest accumulating on their MasterCards from that instant.

Kuma wordlessly served the next customer. She didn't say much to me either, though we stood so close together, but did volunteer that her three children lived overseas. She was lucky to see them once a year, she said. Maybe she thought of them with secret longing while going through the motions at work. When there was a lull we exchanged places and I operated the cash register until Glenda, the store manager, blew in like a tornado.

That was the first I had seen of Glenda, a bad-tempered woman in her thirties or early forties whose brown hair stood on end, even before she yelled at Siham, the afternoon supervisor, because Mary and I were handling the registers rather than watching. There was some regulation about it from head office which had laid the procedures down to the last letter, without bothering to back its rules with the resources to make them feasible. The whole thing could give you the sense that the company bosses operated in some kind of vacuum. Perhaps they were the ones who believed that marketing the brand mattered more than the shambles that lay behind it.[5] Perhaps they seldom left the sanctity of their own comfortable offices to stumble over the goods piled on the floor of the Store. My sources had told me instead that the company was inflexible. But it was hard to feel sorry for Glenda, whose response to the pressures from head office seemed to be to put pressure on her underlings. 'I've told you before,' she shouted at Siham, loudly enough to be heard by half the people in the Store.

Next morning, after Glenda chewed out the supervisors again for failing to test us on the manual, Linda offered to go over it with me. I said I remembered only a little of what I'd read in the out-of-date manual. Stung by this criticism, as if it reflected on her rather than on the management, Linda said we were supposed to spend eight hours reading it and we then went through it in four. The only way to spend eight hours reading it was to do so in your own time, I said, too cross to heed the danger of arguing with Linda, one of the supervisors who handed out shifts, which gave her considerable control over my future in retail.

There was no test on the manual in the next five weeks, but the day of judgment was at hand – I was rostered to work in the fitting rooms on Saturday, the day after my last day of training. Marge, the amiable older woman who did the job on weekdays, assured me there shouldn't be any problem: all I had to do was count the pieces of clothing taken into the fitting rooms, hand out tags numbered one through five, the maximum number of items customers were allowed to take in with them, then match the number of clothes to the tags on the way out, hanging up the clothes the customers dropped on the counter. It sounded simple enough, and by chance there was just one person trying on clothes when I met Marge on Friday afternoon. If it did get busy the next day, she said comfortably, the sales staff would help to put things away. I left the place without giving it another thought, glad to be out of there.

A friend had offered me a spare ticket to the theatre. I was still catching up with old friends, breaking out of the constraints of my project as if I were on vacation. If only it were as easy for workers on minimum wages to throw off the shackles and have a holiday from hard times. Figures released by the Australian Bureau of Statistics in 2001, quoted by the authors of *Fragmented Futures*, showed that 45 per cent of the poorest fifth of the population could not afford a holiday for at least one week a year. A third of them could not afford to have a night out once a fortnight.

The people filing past my counter the next morning had 29 fitting rooms to choose from. Most were occupied by midday. I was already frantic after spending half an hour whipping between the desk where people dumped the items of clothing they had tried on and the overflowing racks around me. Clothing piled up on the little counter as I searched for a clothes-hanger for trousers which were size 20 long, a quest interrupted again and again as more people turned up clutching armfuls of garments or shopping baskets full of crumpled-up clothes. I gave them their tags, then resumed the search for a hanger for another pair of trousers big enough to use for a bedcover. There was a wheelie bin full to the brim with hangers in regular sizes but no regular-sized people. Instead, there were more size 22s waiting for their tags. I rushed back to the desk, then to a rack that was threatening to topple over, while the desk piled up with men's trousers with improbable numbers like 89 and 97 that didn't mean anything to me and, in any case, looked like sliding off the desk at about the time the rack fell over and crushed the little size six standing there waiting for a fitting room. How could there be 29 cubicles and none to spare? I gave up on the pile of trousers, hurling the lot into a big plastic tub the person on the first shift had left half-full.

There was clothing from throughout the Store scattered around, with a rack of lingerie flapping behind me, a rack of children's clothing underneath it and women's clothing in un-appetising colours such as mustard brown and pea-soup green to the side. I was mixing things up, putting extra-small women's tops in with the children's clothes, and women's pants on the rack around the corner where the men's trousers were meant to go. Customers were queuing behind an old woman leaning on a stick, back for the fourth time with another cellophane pack of underpants she wanted me to open so that she could try them on. I had no idea if the Store allowed customers to try on underpants and I wasn't about to check. There were queues in and out of the fitting rooms. I had run out of the tags with the number three, the one problem Marge had warned me about. If the threes ran out, there were always plenty of tags with two on them, she said. I couldn't see the sense in it, when there were so many people whizzing past I had no hope of distinguishing the real twos from the twos that were really threes. Then again, I couldn't see the sense in allowing the place to run out of something as basic as security tags. The Store, like a reformatory for bad goods, seemed to be in a constant state of upheaval. Perhaps that was why so few customers tidied up after themselves. The disarray all around liberated them to drop the clothes in front of me, rather than taking them back to where they came from.

'Oh, please put them back on the hangers,' I begged a tall man in his thirties, who had tried on several pairs of trousers. He handed them straight to the woman waiting for him under the fitting room sign and she started matching pants to hangers. 'No, don't you do it – he needs the practice,' I said. She laughed and handed him a pair.

The Russian woman I attended to next produced fifteen size 18 DD bras, and, taking in the five that were flesh pink, a strangely obtrusive colour on a bra big enough for a traffic cone, thrust the other ten at me as if I were a coat-stand. What was it about trying on clothes that made women lose all sense of proportion? A woman with streaming hair that took up as much room as she did had just wheeled in a shopping cart full of clothes and started riffling through it at leisure, forcing other customers to step around her, holding up garments for my inspection. I had quit looking for hangers, dazed by all the traffic. I felt like I was in a cartoon, drowning in a sea of clothes. The rack of women's clothing was full, but no one came to empty it or wheel it away. I had no idea who was supposed to do it. 'They're very helpful,' Marge had said, vaguely indicating the world beyond the fitting rooms.

But the only sales assistants to be seen were teenagers. The obliging boy who at last dragged the rack of men's trousers away told me he was studying engineering. Another student asked me to call something over the intercom for her. 'It's my first day,' she said in fright when I told her to do it herself, so I gave in. The schoolgirl working in Lingerie came in, looked round-eyed at the rack full of bras and wandered off again empty-handed, but told me they had simply stuck her in Cosmetics on her first day.

I was starting to see why management thought nothing of installing someone who had just finished basic training in the fitting rooms on a Saturday. When I managed to check the cubicles, towards the end of my shift, I found scattered heaps of clothing. The security system had been breached, which was hardly surprising given the number of people who had rushed past me. Feeling like I had been through some kind of blitzkrieg, I hurtled through the racks of bras and into the staff area to clock off, noticing only that management had put up more of the signs about shoplifting cutting into company profits. It was no secret that low-end, high-turnover stores reduced costs by slashing staff numbers, but that didn't make the indifference any less noticeable.

At 10.30 on Monday morning Siham phoned to ask if I could work a long shift that day, from 11.30 until five o'clock. That gave me less than twenty minutes to get ready and hop in the car. I couldn't have made it if I'd had to get to Middleton by public transport. I agreed. It was said that if you knocked back a shift, even on such short notice, you might wait a little longer for the next call from the supervisor. I wasn't ready to risk it yet. I needed the experience, such as it was. I rushed in, then spent the day as a stopgap, relieving people who were taking their lunch-breaks, on security for half an hour or the fitting rooms for an hour, before I was sent back to security again. But I hadn't understood the extent of the uncertainty on offer. Towards the end of the day I asked Linda if she could tell me when I would get another shift. 'No,' she said flatly. Unless the budget provided for more staff, I was on standby. 'It's only that Marge was sick. We've got our full complement.'

If I had been depending on the income from the Store, I wouldn't have known from one week to the next if I would earn a cent.[6] While the job-seekers at the top of the pile were lured with children's school fees and company shares, car leases and laptops, casuals were denied the basic benefits that had accrued during the previous century's improvements in working conditions. The Store's casual employees were denied sick pay and holidays, which meant they came in sick if they needed the money badly enough. They didn't get anything but grief if they missed a shift because a kid was sick or a relative had died.[7] The Store's retail agreement I picked up said that casuals weren't entitled to parental leave, bereavement leave, or leave for jury duty or natural disasters. If they missed a shift to help out in a bushfire or a flood, they wouldn't get jack shit from the Store. The big retailers were shrugging off community responsibilities as fast as they had shrugged off responsibility for the casuals soon to comprise half the industry.

The Shop, Distributive and Allied Employees Association, which had negotiated the retail agreement, had a very cosy relationship with big business. While we were in the training room filling in forms, Sam had told Mary and me that the Store encouraged employees to join the union. When larger groups of employees went through training, the Store gave the union half an hour to sign them up, then deducted union dues from their pay packets (an arrangement some unions call check-off). It was obvious what the company got back – the union was so cooperative one struggled to remember the last time there was a peep out of shop assistants increasingly contending with split shifts and shorter call-in times.

The company's hold over casual employees was a reversion to the days 70 or 80 years ago when men went to union halls and wharves and stood around waiting to see if they would get work that day. The big retailers had tidied up the process so that management barely had to deal with the messy human element. They just left you waiting at the other end of the phone.

In Australia more than a quarter of all employees are casual.[8] There is no other country in the world with so many casual workers.[9] The employers pushing the process insist that they can't compete without a flexible workforce, but the flexibility is all on one side. Permanent work is getting to be a thing of the past, especially in retail and hospitality, but precariously employed casuals are on permanent standby, unable to make so much as an appointment in advance without the prospect of cancelling it at the last moment – or reducing their income.

Only to seem eager enough to *deserve* the work, I phoned Siham later that week. 'This Saturday, we are fine. Next Saturday, can you work two to five?' she said, giving me ten days' notice of three hours of work before asking if I could manage on the cash register on my own. I admitted to one or two gaps in my knowledge of voids and suspended transactions, and Siham said maybe I could come in for more practice the next day. She failed to call back. I wondered if it was part of a deliberate strategy to break down new employees, but I didn't have long to worry if the offer of a single three-hour shift in nine days involved an assessment of my future career as a customer service assistant – and a signal that I should look for the next job. The pressure on the supervisors swept all else aside. There wasn't another whisper about training, but the next call from Middleton was at three that day. 'Hello, Liz. This is Linda. I've had someone ring in sick for tomorrow. Do you want that shift? Two to five? On the registers? Okay?'

'Sure,' I said.

I expected to fill in as understudy again, but when I walked in, Sara, a flighty young redhead whose badge identified her as a supervisor, said no one was going on a break – could I open up register one? I agreed meekly enough, but soon regretted it. The other registers had devices that scanned automatically if you waggled the barcode in front of the little window, but register one had a sort of scanning gun with a defective mechanism. Barely able to work it at first, I stood desperately clicking the thing like a pop pistol as the queue at my register grew and grew. The customers tried to help out. 'You have to hold it like this,' said a man buying socks. 'I think you have to hold it lower,' said a man buying pyjamas with cartoon characters all over them for a little boy who looked like Ginger Meggs. 'It might work better if you run it along the numbers . . .' said a young woman. When Carla, the hard-faced bitch from human resources, appeared out of nowhere to snarl that the light over my register wasn't on, I searched high and low until a customer pointed out the switch.

THE STORE

They seemed to draw on reserves of inner calm to compensate for my visible anxiety. Their patience was astonishing, but I was no less astonished by the situation. There were no big shopping bags at my register. The cash drawer had no five cents pieces in it, and the paper roll in the register had run out before I started work which meant I couldn't do anything at all until someone inserted the next roll, an operation that hadn't been included in my 'continuous training'.

I was still struggling with the scanner. Click. Pause. Click. Pause. Click . . . My whole body sagged with relief, seeing $15.95 come up in the window of the register. If it wouldn't work, I had to enter the nine or ten numbers of the barcode – assuming there was a barcode to be found. Every so often a shopper produced an item without an identifying mark on it, like a piece of lost luggage. I would bash the bell for the supervisor, turning towards her podium in the entrance, only to see that she wasn't there. Because there weren't enough sales assistants, the supervisor was constantly rushing off to check the price of another unidentified object.

The training video said that customers were surprised as soon as they walked into the Store, but they may have been more surprised as they ventured further, past the Hallmark cards and Maybelline makeup, baby rattles, blenders and vacuum cleaners, all the way back to Lighting, looking for help.

The layout of department stores had been influenced by the comparatively recent discovery that consumers prefer to reach for and touch things themselves, instead of being guided by shop assistants or forced to ask for items across a counter.[10] The Store obliged by keeping staff numbers right down. You could have wandered around the place for days without bumping into a customer service assistant.

I would stand there looking helpless, hoping against hope that customers would walk out instead of waiting another ten minutes for someone to check the price. But they didn't. People were too triumphant about finding sale items they'd fished out of a bin or pulled off the wrong rack to give up their purchases without a fight. They responded to my helplessness with what seemed to be a reinvigorated determination to go home with the unmarked mauve lipstick, scented candles and lollypop-pink mules: this is what our hunting expeditions have come to. They seemed almost resigned to waiting, as if the most tiresome parts of the process could be rationalised as part of the pleasure they got from shopping, as they filled whole carts with stuff they picked up almost without thinking about it. The fact that some of the goods were cheaper than in the department store on the other side of the mall licensed the small thrill of consumption. In fact, some things were so cheap I might have wondered at the cent or two of sweated labour that went into sewing the trackies that were sold for $8.99 – if I had time for such notions. Someone had just produced an item with a 50 cent sticker over a tag that said $29.95 and if you had hung me up by my heels I wouldn't have known what to do about it.

THE STORE

The checkout lines were lengthening. The Store was more crowded than ever. Sara was missing in action. The kind young bloke at the next register, a student, stepped in again when the scene at my register threatened to dissolve into chaos. 'Can you use the intercom?' he said, as I wheeled about searching for someone to tell me the price of a Spiderman toy before I walloped the howling brat in front of me on the head with it.

I wouldn't have believed that work so monotonous could be so stressful. I did the same things over and over and over again in an atmosphere of impending crisis. Several hours had passed before I stopped long enough to take off the sweater under my jacket, suddenly noticing that I was suffocating. The Store stinted on air as well as basic equipment. The one advantage of working on the cash registers was that I stood closer to the air that was generously recycled through the shopping centre; even so, I was wrung out. Companies hired casuals for three hours to save giving them a break, or split shifts to make part-time staff pay for their own breaks. If you were on checkout on a Saturday, you didn't lift your head for three straight hours. The big supermarkets had to be worse. In 2004 I would suddenly notice that the staff numbers at my Coles supermarket in Bondi Junction had been slashed. Company management was trying to drive shoppers to the new Coles up the road, using a tactic that temporarily put tremendous pressure on the checkout staff trying to contend with the ever-lengthening lines.

A few minutes before five o'clock, Saturday closing time at the Store, a rude woman whose children were going skiing dumped $273.15 worth of thermals, ski-pants, shades and sunblock on the counter between us. Last came a pair of sunnies without a barcode. I bashed the bell for the supervisor. Linda had taken over from the insubstantial Sara, but Linda wasn't there. I caught sight of Glenda, the store manager, and asked her for help. The kid from Fashion Accessories she grabbed came back with another pair of sunglasses and I scanned them, wincing at the pain in my hand. One afternoon with a broken-down scanner and it had become inflamed. We were into the penalty period. The store was closing. They were checking the take at the other registers. Mine was the last sale all day. I had subtotalled and totalled, entered the Fly Buys number, and pressed the button for credit card purchases. I had slid the credit card receipt over for the woman to sign. 'They're not the right kind of sunglasses,' she said. 'I'm not taking them.'

'I couldn't see any more of the others,' said Fashion Accessories, who was sixteen if she was a day, and we all stood around for a bit. Finally, a supervisor had the wit to say that the shades were a dollar less than the amount I had entered. That meant doing it all again. I waited for mother-of-four to say 'Don't worry about it,' as I would have done at that point if I had three of my four children with me and it was after closing time. 'Why don't you give me a dollar cash?' she said.

It was only after they'd gone that I saw the shopping bag they had left behind. I was all for rushing out after them, but one of my co-workers told me to put the name on the bag and leave it in the pay office for the woman to claim when the Store reopened. I kept forgetting to factor in the changes in the industry since my long-ago days in retail when shopkeepers like my mother gave customers service, instead of just promoting the concept of customer service on training videos.

In those days, circa 1960, when going to the city was an event, my mother would make the trip to the clothing manufacturers dotted about Sydney's Central Railway and the neighbouring slums of Surry Hills to find an outfit for a good customer faced with an occasion. Because most people bought only a handful of new things each year, every aspect of the exchange had more meaning than it does today, with people buying garments by the cartload. One could only suppose the woman was livid when she got home to find herself missing thermals and trackies galore, but, by and large, customers were so accustomed to the absence of customer service that you only had to tell them the tag was missing for them to gulp a mouthful of air and go into the Store again, to dredge up another pair of fake-fur slippers or Bart Simpson underpants, rather than waiting ten minutes for a teenager whose mind wasn't on the job to fail to find them.

Linda was at my register sorting out the cash drawer. 'You did well,' she said, much to my surprise. 'This is the worst register.' I was too grateful for the compliment to ask why the last one through the door got the bung register, and so drained I developed a headache that wiped out the next day.

The next time I went to work, I picked up my first payslip. I learned that casual employment at the Store had one thing going for it, if only one: a casual rate of $19.06 an hour. Although about half of all casual employees believe they get a casual loading, the loading doesn't necessarily compensate for forgone benefits. Some casuals are employed for years at the lowest classification, while permanent employees move up the salary scale – or are paid on a different basis.)[11] My gross pay was $624.25 less $80 in tax. I hadn't said a word about the tax-free threshhold, concluding I would rather argue with the faceless men and women of the tax office than with Tina, the short, beetle-browed Store cashier, who seemed to be off her meds, ricocheting around her cashier's cage in a rage if the money we bundled up at the end of the day included a $5 note facing the wrong way. So I pocketed $544.25, feeling almost rich, until I remembered that my 32 and three-quarter hours were spread over almost three weeks, and included the three days of training.[12] I had earned about $200 a week, $33 *less* than the government benefit for a single unemployed person receiving the maximum rate of rent assistance. (If I were on Newstart, I could earn just $62 a fortnight before my payment was reduced at 50 cents in the dollar; if I earned more than $142 a fortnight, the dole payment would be reduced at 70 cents in the dollar.) It was nowhere near enough to live on for anyone renting in Sydney, where properties for under $180 a week in the least desirable suburbs were near to uninhabitable, according to a newspaper report around that time.[13] The record of expenses I had kept since the previous year petered out the week I picked up my first payslip from the Store. I couldn't see any way of matching my income to my expenses. The alternative was to request a change of status to part-time instead of casual, and return to the iron economies of $13-something an hour – trading off the $6 an hour difference for a more predictable existence, even a measure of the job security that casuals were denied. Part-time work was no guarantee you would earn enough to live on, of course.

I had discussed the subject with a co-worker, a lad of nineteen or twenty with thick black hair and a five o'clock shadow, who was sitting at the big table in the staffroom on his own, looking forlorn. He said he had applied for a full-time job but the Store had given him five half-day shifts instead. That made him typical of the growing number of young people faced with the prospect of working poverty because they couldn't get full-time work – as if it were a commodity too valuable to throw away on the young.[14] His bills were mounting up, because he had to make regular payments, like the $70 a month he owed Optus for his mobile phone, and he was $800 in debt, he said. The one thing to be said for the situation was that he was working regular hours. But the big retailers had found a way to treat some employees as casuals without paying the casual rate, employing them on a part-time basis with a 'flexible' schedule for as little as a single shift a week.

My own relations with the company had entered a phase perfectly characterised by another casual – a nurse – who told researchers: 'They either love me like a rash when they want me to work, or they don't even want to talk to me.'[15] On the Monday after my lost weekend, Siham called at 10 am to ask if I could work that day. I said I had commitments. I had arranged to see the editor of *The Australian* to ask him for an additional three months' leave without pay. (I was away from the paper for one year, including ten weeks' holidays I had accrued, which allowed me to supplement my savings with ten weeks' holiday pay – the sort of security blanket no casual worker could ever have.) Then I was meeting a colleague for lunch. When I started work at the Club, I stopped seeing all but a few old friends in case the consolations of the old life distracted me from the new. There had been no distractions in Greendale, but I was achingly lonely. I saw friends one night a week in Melbourne and stepped up the social schedule in the weeks I did shifts at the Store, where working as a casual gave me the feeling of coming and going like a wraith, as if I might disappear altogether.

The ninth or tenth time I charged past the racks of bras in my black and white shop assistant clothes to clock on, a young man said 'Excuse me' as if I was a customer trying to infiltrate the staff-only area. I liked to think I made an impression on people, but I seemed to have made about as much impression as a doorknob. I could have clocked in ten more times without anyone remembering I worked for the Store. I hadn't clapped eyes on Mary since we'd finished our training. When I enquired, Linda said Mary had returned to Ireland because her father was ill – an excuse too familiar for me to believe it, as if becoming a liar oneself made one less likely to believe others. I could only hope that Mary had conjured up an ailing parent after finding a better job. She was keeping something to herself. We had lunched together again on our second day. The supervisor seemed to think we were old friends because we had said hello. The food court was redolent with the popcorn butter smell that permeates most malls, making you feel hungry, though you know it's some kind of chemical. Mary wouldn't accept anything; all she had for lunch was a bag of chips. Her life was a closed book. I gathered she thought of working for the Store as a last resort, but that was about all she revealed before she slipped off without a word, reinforcing my impression that relations between people who worked for the Store were almost incidental.

Wherever they live and whatever they earn, women often mention the social benefits of work before they mention the benefits of earning an income.[16] People value the social life of the workplace so highly, most say they would work even if they had a reasonable income without it.[17] Social interaction may be one of work's positive pleasures, but there was little schmoozing at the Store. People came and went as if doing the same jobs on the same shifts failed to create a bond. It hardly seemed possible that social connections could be so fragmented unless there was an element of deliberation by the employer (as if management preferred it if employees spoke to each other as little as possible). The weaker the bond between individual employees, the stronger the company's hold. The students filling in a shift or two a week at the Store chattered to one another like normal people, but other staff seemed to have a switch-off button they switched on to go to work. The checkout staff who worked on weekdays were middle-aged women of ethnic backgrounds who betrayed most ethnic stereotypes by being almost eerily detached from the people around them. I recognised the women who had been on the registers the day I started training, but if I spoke to them most stared back blankly, as if they had never seen me before.

I went to the staffroom before or after shifts to talk with other employees, but as a casual coming in at different times each week I seldom saw the same faces twice in a row. Unless I ventured a remark, I sat in silence, conscious of my isolation. I am driven by both temperament and training to try to connect with people, but the atmosphere of the Store was so draining and its procedures so impersonal I did fourteen or fifteen shifts without having a conversation of any length with anyone. I swiped cards, pressed keys and shovelled goods into bags, like a Store-designed robot with a limited set of functions – the functions that define much of the work available in retail, the fastest growing occupational category of recent years.

Some shoppers responded in kind, pushing their purchases at me and squeezing out a single 'thank you' at the end of the operation. The older ones, though, liked to exchange a few words: they still thought of shopping as a social activity, rather than the wordless acquisition of purchases the big retail chains had managed to make it. The youngest ones were restless. Small children tugged at the display boxes on the checkout counter, or ducked under it. I kept noticing the number of distressed toddlers and tearful, hungry babies being dragged around. But all but the smallest were learning to be avid, expectant consumers, a larger part of the process of socialisation than it was a generation ago. There were small children who had spent so much time in shops they knew the procedures better than I did. People would buy their children eight or nine outfits at once, distracting them from boredom by buying them more stuff. Troubled by the thought that the generation who bought clothes by the shopping trolley load would see them as disposable, I tried it on a good-humoured customer with a squadron of children. The clothes wore out about the time the kids outgrew them, she said, unfazed.

'Do you know how much this is?' I said to customers who looked as if they didn't have two coins to rub together, holding up a bottle of makeup or a mascara wand they might find on sale for less in almost any chemist's. Whether or not the $10 trackies were loss leaders, the accessories and makeup more than made up for them.

I had the occasional triumph. 'This card is $8!' I said in shock, to a little old lady in tennis shoes pushing an empty stroller – as if she had lost a grandchild or was preparing to steal one. 'I couldn't see the price,' she quavered, putting away her purse. I directed her to the news-stand upstairs that sold greetings cards for a dollar and off she went with her stroller, leaving me smiling to myself for once.

The exchanges with customers were the best part of the job, but the job was getting to me and my body was starting to let me down. My right hand had been swollen for a week after another short tussle with a scanner gun. I woke some mornings with it bent like a claw. I assumed that the inflammation the chemist's assistant in Greendale had misdiagnosed as carpal tunnel had flared up again, threw down some aspirin and later mentioned the problem to Carla. 'I had it before, when I worked in a factory,' I said, to let her know that I wasn't planning to sue for worker's compensation. I had mentioned it in case I needed her to back me up when I refused to use the scanner again. If Carla had been less interested they would have had to revive her. 'Just speak to the supervisor,' she said down the phone line, her voice so bored I nearly fell asleep myself.

The supervisor on my next shift but one was a stocky blonde with big hair and a generous bust. The name-tag on it said 'Belinda'. I greeted Belinda with the news that I would not work on a register with a scanning gun. The other times I refused, the supervisor had moved another employee to the register I was unwilling to operate. The others all did as they were told, meek and quiet as lambs. Belinda was clearly annoyed by my refusal to do the same. 'You're five minutes late,' she snapped, provoking me to point out that the clock in the store entrance was ahead of the clock where we punched in.

'But *this* is the one we go by,' she said, as if the argument was closed. Who in their right mind would argue with a supervisor whose assessment could influence the next offer of a shift? Me. I snapped back that I would make it up at the end of the shift. There was always a little last-minute shopping frenzy, then the money from the register had to be checked and bundled up, the clothes-hangers put away, the goods discarded at the cash register taken to another counter, and ten minutes of your time had gone – ten minutes or more of overtime the Store stole from me and from every other low-ranking customer service assistant.[18]

Belinda said nothing more, but when she rushed off somewhere, her name-tag bouncing about like it was going on holidays, a boy on a nearby register, a lively red-haired kid with a mischievous grin – a *normal* person – told me that he had worked for the Store the previous year. He was in the Layby Department, which meant staying behind for as much as an hour after the Store closed, without being paid for it. The company paid him for the shift he had been allocated, rather than for the hours on the time-clock, stealing hours of his time, though other students working part-time for the Store couldn't get enough shifts to get by.

To put myself in a better position to find out how the Store treated the casuals who constituted the faster-growing half of its workforce, I tested the system after establishing my cred as a checkout chick. I asked Carla if I would get work only if permanent part-time staff were sick. 'It depends which promotions we've got on,' she said.[19] Then Siham called to say that someone was going on holidays – could I work Wednesday, Thursday and Friday? I quickly agreed. I imagined she meant the following week, which would give me one last chance to look around before I quit to find a job in a nursing home. But I'd misunderstood. Siham was talking about three days' work in sixteen days' time. It would have been ideal if I had a little job like knitting or papier-mâché puppet-making to do at home while waiting for the next call from the Store. But I didn't. I won't be available then, I said. Siham asked, a little resentfully, if I had another job. She hadn't asked me another thing in four weeks, except if I was available for a shift, but she seemed to be suggesting I was letting the side down. It gave me great pleasure to say I *had* to find another job because I wasn't getting the work I had expected from the Store.

The contempt shown to casuals was breathtaking. I was still wondering how people contended with it when the researchers from the University of Adelaide supplied some answers. The casuals they interviewed felt they were treated poorly but had no comeback because they could also be dismissed without warning. 'Most commonly they mentioned a lack of respect,' said the authors. 'I think you are used and abused,' said one casual worker. 'I think they have the attitude we're disposable,' said another, a security guard employed through a labour hire firm. 'If we're not happy with it, they don't give us another shift.'[20]

I worked one more shift, but I was phoning nursing homes by the time Siham left another message enquiring when I would be available again. *Never*, I told the woman on the switch. 'If you're never going to come in again, you have to resign,' she said, insisting that the only way to resign was to write to Carla in human resources. 'Sure,' I said. As if.

Chapter 6

THE HOMES

A WEEK AFTER I started phoning nursing homes, I landed a casual job at Starholme, in far-flung Northwest Hills. The names are fabricated, like the names of the other nursing homes in this chapter. Northwest Hills was in a notch of Sydney's Bible Belt where real estate was appreciating rapidly enough to restore the faith of unbelievers. The neighbourhood was still resolving its identity, so there were big new brick homes with triple garages and high iron railings next to modest cottages.

Starholme looked like a normal family home – but for the 'No entry' sign against the balustrade. The impression of normality was dispelled when I went inside. Two of the nine elderly people in the big front room were tied to their chairs. Others sat in frozen attitudes, as if their bodies no longer obeyed any of the ordinary commands. The very faint smell of urine that hung in the air was more noticeable deeper inside the nursing home.

I was shown around by Delia, the director of nursing, a tall, thin woman with a wide mouth and a thick mop of hair, like a broom turned the wrong way round. She was friendly but distracted. Starholme, like her, seemed slightly disorganised. In the larger rooms one or two tiny women with hands like claws were curled up in the foetal position in their beds. In a corner bed in a big room that smelled slightly of shit, a shrunken woman in a crocheted cap was lying with her eyes open and unseeing, holding a doll dressed in baby clothes. I stood transfixed, but Delia had crossed the hallway into a large kitchen and was pointing out some books with safety instructions, as if I had the job already and the kitchen could blow up at any minute. I was wondering whether to tell her I couldn't cook, but Delia was heading out of the kitchen, through a childproof gate and down some stairs into a laundry. The small room behind was heaped with bulging black garbage bags. 'There's a lot of it,' I said politely, but it wasn't dirty washing, after all. Someone had died the previous week and the family hadn't yet picked up the clothes. I never think about death if I can help it, but Delia was only warming to the subject, going out to the backyard, a stretch of concrete with an old-fashioned washing line, to point to a little white shed, Starholme's charnel house. They put the bodies there so the ambulance didn't have to take them out the front way, she said. I nodded, too overwhelmed to ask why a person hired as a domestic needed to know what they did with dead people.

Delia asked me hardly anything but phoned the next afternoon to offer me two days' work a week as a kitchen hand. It was easier than I had thought it would be to pick up a few days' work a week, but if I were to try, once again, to measure basic living expenses against what I could earn as a casual in a nursing home, I would need a second job – and I needed it in a hurry. I had to be back at the newspaper in about five weeks. The nursing homes listed in the phone book included an establishment called Restwell, which had closed, aptly enough, and one that had become a funeral home. 'Telecom gave me this number,' its director said, sounding defensive. I called dozens more. Many had vacancies for assistants in nursing – who are called personal care attendants in every state but New South Wales – but said I would need a certificate. (While more and more nursing homes expect assistants in nursing or personal care attendants to undertake a three-month course at TAFE for their minimum-wage jobs, there is no hard-and-fast legal requirement – in reality, *anyone* can walk in off the street to work as an attendant in a nursing home.)

I rushed off to the few homes that had vacancies for domestics, visiting one in a flat Sydney suburb in a special gale zone of its own, where even hardy oleanders grew at a discouraged angle. Birds were being buffeted about, dogs crept along the pavement with their ears pinned down, and the first old bloke I saw doing a runner in his bedroom slippers was nearly blown back into the home. I escorted him inside. 'This is ridiculous,' he said with authority, feeling in his pockets as if there might be a key there after all.

The staff were at a meeting that was running late. I left the waiting room after an hour, unable to bear it any longer. I had witnessed a terrible silent drama between a mother and the daughter about to leave her in the home. They tried to pretend that everything was normal. 'Isn't that a nice poster . . . those green trees there,' the mother said in a small, genteel voice before her anxiety overcame her again and she asked who they were seeing and why they were waiting there. The daughter, a big, strong-looking woman in a flowered skirt, kept stealing glances at me to see if I was paying attention. I did a runner myself and spent the rest of the day on the phone.

A church home where I'd left a form had called. Since the institution was a few kilometres from Starholme in a suburb speckled with nursing homes, I explored the possibility of moving into the area. But finding somewhere cheap to rent on the spur of the moment was a challenge that I failed. My search for a caravan park provided final proof of the disjunction between Sydney and the bush. Out there was the infinite-seeming space that made us so nervous about our claim on the land we had stolen. But in Sydney, space was at such a premium that the caravan parks were disappearing faster than common civility. If the phone book was right, there were nine or ten left, and even the few beyond the edges of the metropolis weren't mere caravan parks any longer.[1]

'We're all upmarket now,' said the woman from the 'van park' near Windsor, a historic town lapped by the fast-flowing tide of suburbia. When I was a child, it was where you went for a Sunday drive. I pictured a caravan near a field dotted with cows, but cows wouldn't fit on the ribbons of grass between the McMansions. The woman from the van park said that traffic going towards the city was already choked up by half-past six in the morning, not that I was to be affected by it. Though the cheapest of her cabins was $210 a week, she was booked out until Christmas, about five months away. I was still recovering from the news that renting a rough cabin in exurbia would have set me back $200-plus a week when I learned that $200 was nothing. The 'deluxe' cabins in the park near the Lane Cove River rented out for $600. A week. The budget option would have meant getting a caravan towed to a site you rented for about $100 a week, and paying another $160 for the mobile home, your basic caravan.

After calling more caravan parks on the scurfy perimeter, I finally found one that rented out cabins by the week for $183. 'You bring your own bedding, television and heater,' said the dour woman who answered the telephone. Tempting! But her cabins were on the wrong side of town. To get from there to Starholme, I would have had to skirt half of Sydney, a trip of over an hour, which was longer than it took me to drive from the eastern suburbs and scoot up the M2 freeway around seven o'clock the next morning, ten months to the day since my first day at the Club.

It was seven or eight degrees, barely warmer than it had been in mid-winter Melbourne when I had last risen before dawn to get to work on time. I reached the nursing home fifteen minutes early and met the cook, Helen, a fair-haired woman in a pink uniform and trainers who had worked at Starholme for seven of her 27 years. Darren, the usual kitchen hand, was there to train me to do his job. I warmed to him right away. A gangling jug-eared man in his mid-thirties, Darren had a greeting for everybody as he sprinted through the nursing home with a rattling trolley, distributing fresh water jugs and clean glasses. I followed, trying to take it all in. There were about 45 residents. Several were up, sitting in chairs next to their beds, their eyes open, staring at nothing, and one or two shuffled up and down the hallways as if forced to keep moving until they dropped, but most were still in bed. In the ward where the tiny woman was still holding the doll, Darren lowered his voice and said she was 106 years old. He said it with pride, like a sports fan reciting a record. I was filled with horror, though whether it was at the nearness of death or the terrible persistence of life I couldn't have said.

THE HOMES

It's the smell that first assails you in a nursing home, at that hour, before the beds are changed. I took a deep breath in the corridor, hoping not to gag, and tried to keep my mind on the complications of the job. On the face of it, nothing could have been easier than setting down water flasks and glasses on the bedside stands between the few family photographs and sad relics. But death lurked even there. Darren had pointed out two residents, one at each end of the home, who were liable to choke if they tried to swallow water rather than Sustagen, a specially thickened fluid. I tried to memorise their names. 'You'll be right,' Darren assured me as he raced back to the kitchen.

His kindness made a strong impression on me that morning. I had just got out of a place where management's aggressive indifference was mirrored by the unresponsiveness of the older employees. Starholme, it seemed at first, was no more promising. I didn't know what to expect from a home that had hired me without even checking my references. I couldn't have predicted that the care would be infused with tenderness, or that I would soon be singing 'Happy Birthday' and handing out bits of birthday cake which Helen had slathered with strawberry icing and chocolate bits, to residents with twisted bodies they couldn't seem to straighten out – though even the most far-gone brightened at the prospect of a sugar hit.

Before the residents had their morning tea, Helen, Darren and I had ours, going downstairs to join the seven or eight employees sitting outside along from the line of mops and buckets, soaking up the warmth of the pale winter sun. Most were smoking. Helen lit up and gulped in the nicotine before introducing me, explaining that I was going to do Darren's job on his days off. Someone immediately offered me a cigarette. The atmosphere was welcoming. People had shifted around to make space for us, rather than holding on to their little pieces of concrete.

When a friendly, throaty-voiced assistant in nursing (AIN) I'll call Rosa asked why I had taken a job at Starholme if I lived in Bondi, I said I would be moving to a suburb near the home, prompting my new co-workers to share their knowledge of the area. The purple-haired woman from the office told me which way to go to skirt the tollroads because the tolls would be over $10 a day, about what I would make for an hour's work. Darren wistfully asked what it was like living near the beach, as if we were talking about a tropical paradise rather than an overdeveloped suburb where rents had soared out of reach of people on low incomes. (The rent on a basic two-bedroom flat in Bondi was about $350 a week – $10–20 less than the take-home pay of a kitchen hand working five six-and-a-half-hour shifts.)

Darren's family had long been settled in the western suburbs of Sydney, which put him in the minority. Helen's parents had emigrated from somewhere in the Balkans, bringing with them the customs of the old country, so they grew vegetables and smoked meat in a smokehouse they built in their big backyard in Sydney. The AINs, women in their thirties, forties and fifties,[2] wore patterned shirts that made them look like bank tellers, but many came from ruined and exotic places. Yasmin, a slender, softly spoken woman of about 30 with dark circles under her eyes and who had been up all night with a sick child, was from Afghanistan, a once-beautiful country she hadn't seen in years and was in no hurry to see again. Rosa was an exuberant Lebanese-Australian who had already told me to ask her for help if there was anything I needed. Myrna was a Fijian-Indian with a loud voice and a slightly belligerent manner, who cheerfully observed that the residents were acting crazier than usual that morning.

The nurses and personal carers on the same shift included Australians and Australian-born Chinese, Indonesians, Islanders and Maoris. I would soon see some racial tensions at another nursing home, but the Starholme employees seemed to get along. An atmosphere of friendliness prevailed, possibly because they were united in their feelings about Vera, the proprietor.

The large corporation that originally owned Starholme had sold it to Vera, who promptly showed her stuff by cutting back staff hours, reducing the eight-hour shifts in the kitchen although residents had to be fed the same as always. Helen and Darren either got through their work in the six and a half hours Vera was paying them for, or did unpaid overtime.[3] Helen and I had already bonded in the kitchen discussing Vera's snide and nasty manner. Vera seemed to think that the people she was paying under-award wages of $13-something an hour to wash pots and stand over steaming cauldrons were taking advantage of her.

I had asked for extra training, which certainly seemed to be called for. It was a job conveniently categorised as 'unskilled' by people whose jobs were so highly 'skilled' they could define the skills required by certain minimum-wage jobs right out of existence. Given that there were few legal requirements for a kitchen hand, Starholme set a very high standard, at least on paper. There was no orientation session, but Delia had given me a manual I was presumably to read in my own time, when I wasn't scrabbling around looking for another job for minimum wages. The manual said I was to '... *deliver quality dietary and catering services to residents within budget and in accordance with resident needs and preferences; maintain safe and hygienic operation throughout total dietary and catering services; oversight supplies and ensure adequate stocks are maintained; rotate stock; follow accepted professional infection control guidelines and practices throughout dietary services operation; plan and prepare meals in consultation with relevant others; manage food service areas; maintain work environment and support equipment; complete required reports and records; and pursue own professional development, enhance skills and knowledge and keep abreast of all changes and professional requirements in relation to dietary services ...*' to name just a few of my stipulated duties.

They hadn't checked me out. They knew nothing about me except that I claimed to have been a cleaner and function waiter. But as Delia informed me the next morning, Vera had refused to pay Darren to give me an extra day of training. It seemed to me that there were very real risks involved. I was relieved to notice that diabetics had been coralled at one table. I would be less likely to hand them death in a dessert dish.

The residents who had managed to totter into the dining room that morning, an hour into my second day in the community services sector, included Mrs M, a twig of a thing in brightly coloured clothing who didn't eat much but swooped down on other people's plates and threw the food around, as she did when I put a dish of scrambled eggs in front of Mr W, a rotund Chinese man at her table. Mr W looked like a wise owl but spoke no English as far as anyone knew, conversing only with the cleaner, who was also Chinese. Helen and I reached the table just in time to separate Mr W and Mrs M, the one still spluttering in Cantonese while the other muttered in Romanian. I escorted Mrs M to her room, further delaying a process that was supposed to run like clockwork.

I had been behind schedule all morning. I was still trundling around with the water trolley when I was supposed to be back in the kitchen. I was late setting the tables and late making the toast. I remembered to fix a single slice with marmalade for a woman with alabaster skin who sat down before anyone else, but forgot all about the fruit juice until the end of breakfast, when I rushed to get it, splashed it about a bit, then poured tea from a huge heavy metal teapot I had overfilled. The tea went everywhere. I belted back to the kitchen for a teatowel. The doorway was blocked by a trolley loaded with dirty dishes, and there were more overflowing trolleys around the dishwasher, on the kitchen hand's side of the kitchen.

Helen was at her sink on the other side, washing pots. I had no idea (and she didn't tell me) that washing pots was my job, not hers. While she peeled potatoes and I scraped plates and loaded the dishwasher, which I would do fourteen times before the breakfast dishes were done, Helen talked about her family, reporting with some pride that her late mother was 'traditional', and had kept up the ways of the old country. Helen had cooked for the family from the time she was ten, however. Her mother insisted on it. While other little girls went out to play, Helen peeled potatoes and chopped vegetables. She was still at home cooking – she kept house for her father. But one night a week she let her hair down and went pub crawling in the city. Exhilarated by doing something wild and crazy, which was out of character, she mentioned it to me several times. Her innocence made me feel protective, but I was the one who needed protecting and Helen went on covering for me for as long as I worked at Starholme.

When we went downstairs the employees outside on their break were being stoic about death, which hovered around the nursing home like a character in an old Ingmar Bergman film. A resident had died on the weekend. Rosa said that she had been about to go into his room when someone else on duty said, 'He's gone.' 'Gone where?' Rosa had said, not knowing. He had gone to his eternal rest before, rather than after, his meal – they usually go after, said another of the carers. They all gave the dead man's daughter a moment's respectful consideration, then it was on to the next subject – traffic fines and cops. Several employees drove as far as I did to get to work, from suburbs way out west where housing was cheaper but jobs were hard to find. They were comparing notes on the spots where the cops lay in wait for the speed hogs. Helen, who sat smoking, said little. I produced the chicken on rye sandwiches I had made before leaving home that morning, and offered them around. I was trying not to think about people dying after eating, a detail that could put you right off your dinner if cooking institution food hadn't already done so. In my case, though, calling it cooking was an exaggeration.

I wasn't a complete failure at the job, just the parts I was paid for. It only took me a day or two to remember many of the residents by name. I stood patiently chatting with them, though patience is a virtue that I lack. Of course, I didn't have to argue with those howling in protest at being escorted to the shower or the toilet, much less clean and change them if they were incontinent, which was what the carers did for their minimum wages. I just wheeled in the tea trolley and stayed talking a moment.

In one room a woman who hadn't stopped complaining at breakfast, saying the toast was too soft, the porridge too lumpy, the tea too sweet and so on, like some mature-age Goldilocks, was quietly lying in bed holding an old photograph album. She wanted to show me (or anyone else willing to pause a moment) a photograph from before the Second World War of her and her siblings as children. She was the only one left, she said. I couldn't see it properly without my glasses and waited for her to read out the names and inscriptions before haring off again. I was supposed to be back in the kitchen, as the pressure built towards the final tense countdown to lunchtime when the makings for 45 meals were set out on individual trays, ladled into the bain marie or carried into the dining room.

Helen's face didn't show much of what she was thinking, but even she looked astonished when I managed to knock over a tray of glasses *and* drop the lids of the bain marie with percussive effects – probably because I started laughing when a glass bounced like mad. I had to be shown how to put together the mixmaster and how to use a certain kind of can opener, exposing basic gaps in my knowledge as a kitchen hand. I thought of telling Helen about my book (as I would, in the end) to explain why I was so hopeless at the job. I could stare at a kitchen in pre-lunch frenzy without a clue as to what to do next. Should I stir the gravy bubbling like Vesuvius, carry another big vat of cooked vegetables from the stove to the sink, or empty the hot water warming the bain marie before spooning in the potato I had just mashed? I had no idea of procedure, and gentle, sweet-natured Helen was no help. Like so many other capable people stuck in menial positions, she lacked the confidence to assert herself. 'I don't like to tell you . . .' she said after another small crisis demanded intervention.

My own problems continued. Helen had asked me to fix the

dessert. Glad to have something definite to do, I flapped about collecting the makings, then found I couldn't lever the lid off the big metal ice-cream container and stood there in an agony of embarrassment, wrestling with it.

When lunch had been served and the dishes loaded into the clapped-out dishwasher another seventeen times, rattling in syncopation with the music from Triple J which blared through the kitchen, I mopped the floor and put out the garbage. I knocked off exhausted 45 minutes after the official end of my shift – 45 minutes for which I wouldn't be paid[4] – changed out of my stained trousers, put on a shirt that didn't smell of sweat and went for an interview at Excelsior, a big church home in the churchy suburb up the road.

In the hallway, a tiny bent woman in a pink cardigan kept walking towards the security doors then breaking into the most heart-rending sobs. 'Oh, they're not here yet, they haven't come,' she cried, in a voice at once childlike and old and cracked.

One of a string of nursing homes run by a religious organisation, Excelsior was very much part of the trend towards corporatisation of what had been a cottage industry. The churches that ran about half of all nursing homes had linked their operations. I had gone from an institution where the cook was close enough to the residents to acknowledge their birthdays, to nursing home care on an industrial scale.

Annette, the administrator of the nursing home, a striking, dark-haired woman with the knack of lavishing all her attention on you at once, which seemed wasteful, explained that Excelsior's residents were demented. 'They have challenging behaviours,' she said, asking if I could cope. I didn't know, I said. I told her that when I had lived in New York, I did volunteer work with the homeless, crack addicts mostly, who could be, uh, challenging, in their own way. It sounded improbable, even to me, and I was there at the time. The truth could be as disappointing as a drink that had gone flat, not that it seemed to matter. But instead of asking me about that experience, Annette only wanted to know if I felt I could deal with demented people. She didn't investigate my feelings about any other aspect of the job, as if one cleaner was the same as another and one cleaning job the same as the next.

Annette called with an offer of work before I reached home. If that was a record, I soon saw why. They would give me shifts only if other employees were sick or on holidays. The one difference with the Store was that Church Homes Inc. didn't spell it out at the start, leaving me to find out for myself that I was on permanent standby again. (If I received government benefits, I would have spent my life recalculating my income – lodging a form every fortnight to declare any earnings in the previous two weeks. You had to declare earnings when you did the work – not when you were paid – even if there was nothing to count on in the weeks between, which made quite a contrast with the people making the rules: the Centrelink senior executives whose salaries had swollen from \$85,888 a year in 1997/98 to \$128,165 by 2003/04.[5])

I ran into Annette on my first shift, when she saw a cleaner bend over to pull out a bed and came in to tell us to follow safe work practices. Until the orientation course, weeks later, I escaped the further notice of Church Homes Inc.'s battalion of managers.

I'd had some bad moments in the past year, usually as the result of my own incompetence, but I touched bottom about an hour after the start of that first shift at Excelsior, when I stumbled across a commode that hadn't been emptied, gagged and rushed out to gulp some air in the corridor. I stood there a minute to remind myself that I would be spending a few days doing what thousands of underpaid workers did every working day.

'This is nothing,' said Nella, who had been assigned to train me. 'You get poo all over a room.' A delicate-featured blonde, Nella had emigrated from Chile with her family at the age of 40 and had started work for the first time. 'Today it's good,' Nella said again, as we carried our mops and buckets from one section of the nursing home to the next and joked about missing the smell of pee when we went home, pretending to sniff around in search of it, as we swept and mopped the next set of bedrooms, pulling beds and potty chairs out from the wall and mopping up the puddles.

Though she did the job conscientiously, Nella detested it. 'Same every day,' she said, filling the bucket and putting in a squirt of 'chemical'. 'Every day the same,' she said bleakly, emptying garbage bags of shit-smeared paper from the stinking bathrooms into the 'contaminated' bin in a yard at the side. If

I were condemned to do this for months on end, I would cry too, as Nella said she did on her first day there.

The linoleum we had to mop stretched to the horizon. I couldn't get the motions right – taking desultory swipes or putting too much of my back into it and hurting my wrist in the process. Nella's bits of linoleum were spotless; mine stayed streaked, as we proceeded from one wing to another to mop around the residents in a big sitting room. I stopped feeling sorry for myself when I saw them.

There were people whose mouths were stretched open and bodies arced in wracked attitudes that evoked a medieval depiction of the torments of the damned. A grey-haired woman who walked bent forward, as if in a storm, asked me what I was doing. I said that Nella was teaching me to clean the place properly. 'I wish I could do it,' she said wistfully, then talked to herself again. People struggled to communicate with some vestige of normality. A bearded man in a wheelchair tried vainly to move out of my way, singing a sort of broken bar or two of a song when I thanked him. I stopped mopping for a minute to talk with a dark-haired attendant about an old lady with clouded, unseeing eyes who was asking for help, softly saying she wanted to go home. 'She thinks her children are at school, and she still has to pick them up,' said Diane, the attendant. The old woman could barely move, but in her mind, she heard the voices of her waiting children.

In the 1970s, a few years before the mental hospitals were

emptied out (leaving helpless ex-patients to fend for themselves – the scandalous, unanticipated consequence of a reform that had seemed so necessary at the time), I visited the back wards of Callan Park, Sydney's best known mental hospital, for a series of articles for a now-defunct newspaper, the *National Times*. I was terribly shocked by what I saw. One young man banged his head against a wall over and over again. Other patients sat on the floor rocking like automatons, as if the effects of institutionalisation were more grievous than the illnesses for which they had been locked up in the first place.

Diane confided that she saw changes in the residents after only three weeks in the home, changes associated with the deprivations of life in an institution rather than the advancing dark of Alzheimers. Sometimes they just wanted attention, she said, but they could never get the attention they had had at home. Certainly not in the sitting room at Excelsior, where Diane's concern for those suffering around her singled her out. Surprised by the tenderness of some of the care at Starholme, I noticed the opposite – indifference – at the larger Excelsior, where some carers sat out their shift paying little attention to the residents unless there was a crisis.

At lunchtime, four hours after the start of the shift, Nella and I joined her friend, Francine, an Indonesian woman in her fifties, who had been in Australia four years and spent her first full day in the country going door-to-door asking for work as a domestic. She cleaned someone's house and accepted $10 for it, not knowing any better. The story was a little difficult to follow. Francine had lost most of her teeth and spoke English with a pronounced accent. The language problems limited what she could do. In her previous job, she had lugged heavy mail bags around, until her failing health made it impossible and she found the job at the home. I saw her gasping for breath late that afternoon as the three of us mopped a smaller sitting room and I said something about it to Nella, who reported that her friend had heart problems but went on working because she needed the money.

Church Homes Inc. employed both women for six and a half hours a day, which cut their salaries and benefits, but was an unintended mercy in its way, since it was hard to imagine work more grinding and disheartening. 'You get used to it,' someone had said that morning when I mentioned the suffocating smell of urine that seemed to surround us. I was sure I could smell it hours after finishing my first shift at Excelsior, though I had swum in a chlorine pool and showered before and afterwards.

There were five cleaners on my next shift. Annette had issued an edict. She wasn't satisfied with the general standard of cleaning. I wore a wrist strap I had bought on my way home the previous evening for a few bucks less than a domestic employed as a casual earned in an hour – $14.86, including a 10 per cent loading for holiday pay and sick pay.[6] I managed to avoid mopping for an hour or two, instead joining the small team cleaning windows and scraping food from the grooves of chairs. I worked alongside a beautiful dark-eyed Syrian woman, by the name of Rana, who told me she had a son of fourteen, the age she was when she married. Michelle, the third member of the team, was a laconic little stringbean in her forties who kept her thoughts to herself until I remarked that it seemed possible to find work in nursing homes from one day to the next; she pointed out that we were talking about casual shiftwork for minimum wages. Michelle was hanging out for a shift that fitted in with her other job in a factory, which had just been cut back to three days a week from the five days it had been for some years. There had been no warning – they just changed it from one week to the next, she said, in the same calm, dry tone, picking up the spray bottle and moving along to attack another section of window.

The glass we were cleaning stretched from floor to ceiling, along a corridor that let out on to a deserted garden. I was cleaning the top part by leaping up, arm outstretched, when a middle-aged woman in a nurse's uniform appeared out of nowhere, watched me for a moment, and then told me to use a chair. I neither knew nor cared if the woman in uniform had the right to give me orders. I was outraged by her assumption of superiority over a mere domestic. 'I'll tell you what,' I snapped. 'You do your job and I'll do mine.'

I took the precaution of reporting the exchange to Cora, the big, loud, lively woman assigned to train me for the rest of the day. She couldn't get over it. 'Tell them what you said,' she repeated whenever she paused to talk to one of her many friends among the carers and the kitchen staff, picking up the thread of a conversation begun the previous day, and switching between English and Hindi. From Fiji, which her family fled after the coup, 30-something Cora had worked at the Home for six years and seemed to have intimates wherever we went. Keeping up with the gossip gave someone as bright as Cora something to think about while mopping interminable figures-of-eight on the interminable lino. I was back to mopping again.

Indeed, the mopping was better than our next task – cleaning the bathrooms. An attendant had just been in the vicinity with a resident in a wheelchair who had done what must have been a world-class dump in his pants. And the tell-tale smell hanging over the corridor was like Chanel No. 5 compared with the smell in the bathroom. Cora hurled herself at the windows and opened them, spraying air freshener around madly, as I waited just outside, considering if it was worse to inhale nosefuls of air freshener or nosefuls of the smell of shit. The air freshener won by a country mile, though once again I wondered about all the chemicals we snuffled up.

On my previous shift at Excelsior the pest control man had whisked past with a squirt gun, spraying roach spray over all the skirting boards. Meanwhile, we cleaners sprayed floors with one chemical we had diluted, wiped another chemical on basins and taps, dumped Domestos in the toilets, and sprayed Windex on the glass and air freshener on anything not yet saturated with product.[7] I said we were probably inhaling things that weren't any good for us, but after all those years of bathroom cleaning, Cora had better things to think about. She just shrugged and sloshed another bucket of water over the floor, as I mopped desultorily, wondering where my former conscientiousness had got to.

I couldn't muster much enthusiasm for mopping and slopping out bathrooms, I said. This was hardly surprising. The real revelation was that one wasn't supposed to say so, even there, in a stinking bathroom, on one's first or second day, as if getting the job on whatever terms was an opportunity not to be dismissed lightly. 'She's a character,' Cora told her friends at lunchtime, when we went out to sit at the plastic picnic table set on a slope on the concrete, where the domestics, nurses and carers took their breaks, even in the depths of winter, the late arrivals clinging to the sides like passengers on a boat that had hit the high seas.

It was evident that Church Homes Inc. was hiring people, rather than laying them off, but my fellow employees behaved as if they were forced to fight to keep what little they had. Rana, who had worked for the organisation for a few weeks, came outside at lunchtime, but nervously checked and rechecked her watch, as if frightened of being caught napping, a fear I would better understand after one more day on the job.

I had already met Bev and Marlene, who worked in the laundry, as I would on my next shift. Forty-something Bev had short white hair, pale, very faintly freckled skin and small, regular features, like an advert for Anglo-Saxon genes. Marlene, a big lump of a woman a few years older, was also blonde and fair. The two had quite a reputation. 'Just be strong down there, is all I can say,' said a fellow employee as I headed for the laundry. On a cold and blustery morning with rain lashing about, Bev was outside having a smoke, complaining to a lantern-jawed maintenance man named Arthur that four of us were to work in the laundry that day. 'It's absolutely ridiculous. We'll be falling over each other.' I laughed, saying it was clear she didn't want us there, but I was given a welcome of sorts after shrugging on the hospital gown she gave me to wear over my work clothes.

While showing me her domain, which had trolleys of dirty laundry on one side of an area marked off with duct tape, the border separating the 'dirties' from the stuff going through the washing machines and rumbling tumble-dryers, Bev claimed that she and Marlene were pleased to hear they were getting an Australian in there. I was born in Holland, I said. 'At least you speak the language,' Bev said. The atmosphere at Starholme had given me the idea that nursing homes were at the forefront of multiculturalism, an illusion that was evaporating faster than the moisture in the mattress protectors swirling around the dryers. 'There are a lot of immigrants in this industry,' I said cautiously. 'It's frigging shocking,' she responded, shaking her head. Rana and Nella, the other members of our team, had started their shift. Bev, who had it in for Rana, had belittled her all morning, claiming she didn't understand English, then complaining that she had paid no attention to her when she worked in the laundry. 'She acted like I wasn't there.'

The Excelsior laundry did the washing for four other institutions. When the maintenance man turned up with a trailerload of dirties from the sister nursing home up the road he caught sight of Rana outside, innocuously pegging something on the clothesline, and popped his head through the double doors of the laundry to contribute his thought for the day. 'She's as useless as tits on a bull,' he said, then filled his trailer with bags of laundry we had washed, dried and folded, and went away again. We started over, dragging another trolley of dirty laundry across the border. 'You can load 'er up,' said Bev. 'Get dressed.' We put on aprons and gloves. While I loaded one machine, Rana unloaded another. 'Get closer to it,' said Bev. Rana stayed where she was. Not sure if she understood less English than she let on, or was too proud to take orders from a bonehead like Bev, I put in my five cents worth, saying she could hurt herself if she dragged things out of the machine with her back bent. 'I know,' she said.

'She gave you The Look,' Bev said fifteen minutes later. Rana had vanished. 'No, she didn't,' I said, earning more looks – disbelief this time – from Bev and her cronies at lunch around the picnic table. I had dug out my lunch and leaned over the tattered old copies of *Woman's Day* on the table to offer the others a radish. 'Are you a vegetarian?' said Bev's friend Lillian, who had used a tanning product that gave her skin a slightly unnatural golden tinge she clearly considered preferable to the cafe-au-lait complexion that nature gave some of our colleagues. Lillian worked in the Excelsior kitchen, where they heated up frozen food prepared in another part of the Church Homes Inc. empire. But Lillian had very firm views about food in general. I had fished out a stick of celery and some rye bread and cheese to offer around. 'No, I like *lunch*,' Lillian said with peculiar emphasis, as if I had offered her reindeer meat and called it dinner. Between the radish and the celery she had informed me that she only bought shallots once in a while (as if shallots represented an extreme of exoticism beyond which she wouldn't go). She ate a piece of Tip Top toasted. *Lunch*.

I was suddenly reminded of lunchtimes at Manly Girls High, circa 1962. Though some of my schoolfriends were revolted by the doorstep sandwiches Mum made me, the same sandwiches inspired others to comment on the main attractions of the culture we immigrants had brought to Australia. Salami, for example. I had informed my companions at the plastic table that I grew up in Manly (one has to say something!) and Arthur had just asked if I went to Manly Domestic, a home science school of that era. It seemed I had only narrowly missed meeting the appealing lantern-jawed Arthur back then. He went to a high school out west, he said, but he and his friends used to meet the girls from Manly Domestic at Fairy Bower and climb under the rowboats. 'The young have no frigging idea,' said Bev. There was the easy laughter of middle-aged people spending a moment reminiscing.

Lillian had mentioned an employee whose hours had been cut back, one aspect of a subject brought up at every break, with employees almost obsessively comparing notes on the rosters as if to make sure they knew exactly where each drib and drab of work had gone, like hungry people guarding their own small stock of food from the marauding hordes. Bev raised it again soon after we went back in to stand together near the doors at the back, sorting clean laundry, throwing the 'personals' into tubs and folding sheets and towels, mattress protectors, blankets, rubber undersheets, face washers, bibs, napkins, tablecloths, pillowcases and dishrags into tottering piles. There weren't any spare shifts in the laundry, she said. Lurching this way and that as I tried to fold a double sheet according to specifications, I suddenly remembered the letter that had been in my possession since I started my shift that morning. It set out the terms of my employment, saying that as a casual I might be requested to work shifts on an emergency or relief basis from time to time, all of which was news to me since Annette hadn't breathed a word about the conditions of my employment. Church Homes Inc. seemed to be topping up the number of casuals on the books, covering all possible emergencies while setting up a kind of contest over working hours.[8]

The work in the laundry was physically demanding. Each time I emptied a machine, tugging like mad at the coiled sheets, I was relieved I had taken up swimming. But emptying a machine was bliss compared with shoving in a load full of soiled sheets and dirty underpants. Observing that Bev felt compelled to stake a claim on the work, I said the office hadn't told me I'd have to fight for shifts, and she assured me I could have plenty of work when people were on holidays. She would be gone herself for three weeks at Christmas, she said. Marlene was going on holiday the month after next, and in the meantime, Gloria in the kitchen was on holiday for a month – maybe I could ask for that shift, if Marilyn hadn't got in first. I could see that Bev felt she should give me some encouragement, if only as a fellow Caucasian, while reminding me that the work belonged to her – and another woman, who was on maternity leave. 'When Betty comes back, there won't be any shifts in the laundry,' she said.

When the alarm went off at a quarter to six the next morning, an hour and three-quarters before I signed in for a shift at Starholme, I woke thinking about a way to speed up my first task of the day. I took so long distributing water jugs through the home that I had fallen behind before the day was properly begun. Accustomed to going at my own speed, I found it difficult to pick up the pace, but that put more strain on Helen, who was already under pressure. I decided to leave the water jugs where they were. Taken to the logical extreme, this solution suggested that I could further improve my performance by scrapping most of my designated tasks. But Helen had hit on the same solution. I no sooner charged into the kitchen than she told me the nurses could deal with the glasses and jugs.

I was too relieved about the tiny reprieve to dwell on the fact that the overworked care staff would have to add a bit of my job to theirs.[9]

It was my sixth shift at Starholme but I still didn't have the routines down, let alone the dietary requirements of the bedridden residents whose meals were set out on trays. I had managed to remember the peculiar requirements of the resident who shouted the house down unless he was given ice-cream for breakfast and lunch, but that wasn't much use – the registered nurse visiting that day saw his plate and surged into the kitchen to voice her objections to his unusual diet. Residents were getting too many sugary things, she said sharply. Helen tried to explain about Ice-cream Man, but was too diffident to argue.

Reticence used to be regarded as a virtue, but it just holds you back nowadays. While the beneficiaries of the new economy excelled, first and foremost, in enumerating the special talents they brought to an enterprise, the workers bundled together in fast-expanding service industries had been unable to capitalise on the growing demand for their labour.[10] Helen couldn't defend herself, let alone talk up her dedication to the job. Though she was never praised, she put heart and soul into it, stopping whatever it was she was doing to exchange a greeting with Rina, a resident who liked to stand just inside the kitchen (which was supposed to be off-limits) rubbing away at an invisible spot on the nearest cupboard, as if the scrap of paper in her gnarled hand was a scourer and she had a role to play. Rina was draped in something that looked like a scarlet curtain. 'You look nice in red,' said Helen, taking the time to be kind even in the midst of the mealtime frenzy, when every second counted. But she made such modest claims for herself, it hadn't occurred to her that she should get more, even if getting more was the defining spirit of the age.

The question came up at morning tea when we joined Aroha, a calm, reflective woman of about 50, employed as a carer by both Starholme and Excelsior. She would race from one to the other, working thirteen hours a day. Excelsior paid about a dollar an hour more, which took her pay there all the way to $13 an hour. (Nearly 50 per cent of all aged care workers and 60 per cent of personal care attendants earn less than $500 per week.[11]) The figures reminded Helen of meeting a man in a bar who said that for a time he had earned the 'insulting' rate of $13 an hour. I couldn't convince her that $13 *was* a low wage by adult standards, and the moment to do so had passed – Helen and Aroha were already talking about people they considered to be over, rather than under, paid, like the young construction workers earning up to $1500 a week. They spent it all and never had anything to show for it, said Aroha, the sole supporter of two of her three children, which helped to explain why she worked double shifts just to get by. I asked what she would do if she earned as much as the construction workers. Aroha grinned. 'Save it, probably,' she said, just as the sun slipped out from behind the clouds as if making its own shy claim on the day. I noticed my ration of weather more when I started work too early to enjoy it.

Basking in the delicate warmth and the pleasures of companionship, we stayed outside a little longer than we should have. 'I didn't know we were down there so long,' Helen said, as if it were all her doing. I mashed the potatoes, adding butter and milk, then drained and mashed the pumpkin, my sweating face hanging over it like the moon, feeling ridiculously proud of myself for remembering a few simple tasks without prompting. But Helen had taken the precaution of bringing in reinforcements. While Yasmin flicked cutlery on to trays, Rosa dished out the desserts. 'We're here to help each other,' she said.

My faith in human nature restored, I returned to Excelsior for a shift with Bev. I had kitted myself out in a hospital gown, apron and gloves, and started sorting the big bag of dirty laundry that had tumbled down the chute, like a message from on high, when Bev sauntered over to inspect my handiwork, remarked on the big load of washing coming in that day, and said something about the 'delicates', like the woollen sweaters and the jackets we washed in a separate machine. Not everyone bothered, but she liked to take extra care with them, she said. It was up to her to remind herself that she did her job as conscientiously as possible. No one else noticed until something went wrong.

But, according to Bev, something *had* gone wrong and Rana

was to blame – not that Rana was mentioned by name. '*She* left the dryer on. *She* said it wasn't her . . .' Two more bags had bumped down the chute, distracting Bev, who counted up the morning's tally before remembering another atrocity *she* had committed. Rana was nowhere to be seen, which was fortunate. At morning tea, several others joined in. It was like watching chickens peck the sick one to death.

Bev herself was gone by mid-afternoon. With three hours of my shift left, I was in the laundry folding things, half-listening to ABC Radio instead of the usual commercial station, day-dreaming about my day off, when Annette appeared and asked me to go to the orientation session the next day. The arrangements must have been finalised days earlier, but no one had mentioned it to me until that moment, as if any appointments I may have made were as insignificant as I was. My first impulse was to refuse but I thought better of it, deciding to go to the session to make my sudden departure the following week more convincing (as if anyone would notice).

The training room was directly opposite the laundry. Instead of standing on concrete all day we trainees got desks and chairs and folders of material to take home, as if we could all dream of being conference-goers some day. In fact, Church Homes Inc. did us proud, with a thick pile of folders and a handbook for employees and volunteers complete with religious quotations.

The most interesting revelation to me was that a multimillion-dollar corporation with a couple of thousand employees and a bunch of nursing homes spread around the nation could count on the competitive advantage of volunteer labour.[12] Church Homes Inc. was paying me and my fellow employees $13- to $14-something an hour to mop floors and baby-sit frail aged people with senile dementia, but they had people willing to do it for less – believers – as well as family and friends of residents.[13] 'Isn't it interesting that this large corporation has all this unpaid labour,' I said and got a look from Deidre, the trainer, a brisk woman with a basin haircut.

The handbook said we were expected to conduct ourselves in a manner that promoted the organisation's Christian values. I had spent my time in the laundry swearing like a trooper, as I often do, prompting Bev to advise me that there were times you could swear and times you couldn't. I gathered that swearing was out at the training session. Soon after handing out the folders, Deidre said: 'We don't have only [and here she named the particular Protestant denomination the homes were associated with], we have many other good Christian people.' I said nothing, for a change.

Deidre and I hadn't hit it off from the beginning. I believe she expected a little more humility from someone in my position. The six other trainees included two Chinese women who would work with the nursing staff while completing tertiary studies, a stolid aged care nurse whose own mother was in a home (and loved it, she told me), and a middle-aged woman with a big laugh and a body to match who said she was a former director of nursing re-entering the industry to work part-time. We had introduced ourselves in turn. 'I'm a domestic,' I said. 'I've had a few shifts here cleaning and doing the laundry. The laundry's better.' I was repeating something Nella had said. 'You see,' she'd said as we folded sheets on my first day in the laundry, nodding towards the double-width doorway. 'The laundry's better. You've got the door, the radio . . .' The thought that Nella spent her working life with so little to sustain her had brought tears to my eyes. The words didn't have the same effect on Deidre, who had decided to put me in my place.

The organisation expected 'continuous improvement' from each person, she said. '*Even* if you want to be in the laundry.' Fuck her hat. '*Want* may be putting it a bit strongly,' I said, wondering if she was even aware she was patronising me.

Nurses use a lot of jargon – if she used jargon we didn't understand, we should stop her, Deidre said, provoking a burst of whispering from the Chinese women. Their English was uncertain. One was clearly finding it difficult to follow the trainer, who spoke so rapidly that her words tumbled over each other. 'Facilityiswhereyouwork,' she said, glancing at me. I obediently wrote it down. I hadn't been orientated in the first 55 years of my life and here I was at 56, getting orientated for the fourth time in eleven months.

Whatever was happening to low-wage workers unable to find anything but casual shiftwork doing shitwork, the training industry was growing apace as employers who had once been responsible for giving workers full-time jobs and sick leave hired casuals and showed them videos about the effects of hard physical labour because (1) the law required it, and (2) they were getting sued. The increasingly tenuous relationship between employers and employees worked both ways; more and more nurses were suing nursing homes over injuries sustained while lifting and moving residents.[14] 'Whether you're a nurse or a cleaner in the laundry, because you prefer to be, occupational health and safety is for you,' said the trainer. The strain on your wrists from a day spent mopping institution linoleum went unmentioned, in fact, as did the physical wear and tear of emptying industrial-sized washing machines. But we spent a quarter of an hour in the ice-cold training room on the importance of washing our hands. If there was one person in Australia who didn't need a lecture on hand washing, it was me. I sometimes had to remind myself it wasn't cool to ask grown-ups if they had really washed their hands after going to the toilet. If all else failed, I could soon start giving hand washing classes myself.

First water, then fire. Deidre had put on a video about what to do if there was a fire – and with so many good Christian people in the home, one could only hope to Christ there wasn't one. At Excelsior there were four members of staff on duty at night to contend with about 60 residents with some form of dementia, a vast improvement on staffing arrangements at night in some other nursing homes.[15]

But for every nurse gone from the premises, there were several more managers, the same as in any other industry where the grunts who did the maintenance and the heavy lifting were being replaced by serried rows of suits. The formal training session over, we were inspecting a nearby nursing home, like tourists in the Land of Nod, when Deidre, our tour guide, spotted an acquaintance. I should have guessed I'd be exhibit number one. 'This is Liz, who likes to work in the laundry,' she said. I reminded myself I would have the last word. Making some excuse, I farewelled my fellow trainees and hit the tollroad, heading home to make notes, the real work of the day.

I didn't have much time left. I had to be back at the newspaper the following week, so I engineered an encounter with Vera, who hadn't shown up at Starholme while I was there. Contacting her at another of her nursing homes, I claimed I was calling because the two people working in the kitchen couldn't finish the work in the six and a half hours she paid them for, and thus were working unpaid overtime. But Vera had persuaded herself that she was the injured party in all her dealings with her employees. 'It doesn't matter what I've done for them, they want more time . . .' She said she had hired a consultant to set up the program to minimise possible sources of food contamination in the kitchen of the home. It was a standard industry program, known as Hazards at Critical Control Points (or HCCP), but Vera was managing to suggest that she had set it up at Starholme purely to lighten the load of employees too shiftless to help themselves. 'All they want is more and more, and they don't put anything into it.' I might have imagined there was a shred of truth in what she said, if I hadn't been there to see for myself.

Rather than sacking me on the spot, Vera kept throwing insults around. Twenty minutes into it, I told her she was unfair. I had called, I told her, because I believed she had made a mistake when she cut the hours of the kitchen staff. But I could deal with it, I said (forgetting that I had to deal with it for two more shifts at most). I could work the six hours a day and go home leaving some things undone. It wasn't *my* nursing home, I said, stopping just short of pointing out that getting the place certified every third year wasn't my problem, but hers. At last I had got under her thick hide. 'The duties on that job routine should be completed. If you can't manage the jobs you've got, then you can't have the job.'

There was a message from Vera on my mobile the next day, asking me to call her. Wondering if I ought to drive all the way to Northwest Hills the next morning only to learn that I'd been sacked, I tried to reach her but heard no more.

I went to work in high spirits. Before I skipped into the dining room to set the table, I reported part of the conversation to Helen. I hoped to make her stand up for herself the next time, but she wouldn't do anything of the kind. It wasn't in her nature and, besides, she liked it where she was.[16] But the news of my set-to with the boss had caused considerable excitement.

'Good on you,' said a registered nurse, clapping me on the back. The personal care workers flocked to the kitchen to ask what was going on. Vera had called Rosa to ask her to work in the kitchen, then changed her mind. A broadly smiling Rosa insisted that if Vera tried to sack me, I should refuse to go. Instead, I admitted that I would be leaving after one more shift. When Delia appeared, looking worried, saying she had something to tell me, I got in first. 'Tomorrow will be my last day,' I said impulsively, to spare her further embarrassment. She had never been anything but kind to me. It was only after I had spoken that I told myself I should have shut up and waited to be sacked for daring to speak out. It would have been a great ending for my story.

It wasn't the end, however. I learned something more about the fortitude of my fellow employees the next day when I joined Aroha, Yasmin and Helen out in the yard and we talked about Yasmin's birthplace, Afghanistan. The only time she'd gone back for a visit, sometime in the 1990s, the mujahadeen were in control and women had to cover themselves to go out. She couldn't get used to it again, she said. 'Of course, it was even worse under the Taliban.' Her relatives had told her it still wasn't safe – not that she had any intention of ever going there again. 'Can you believe our government is talking about sending the refugees back?' I said[17], not sure how the others would respond. I was touching on the issue then said to divide privileged middle-class people like me from battlers like them. But there was no division. Aroha observed proudly that New Zealand, her homeland, had taken in some of the refugees from the *Tampa*. Not even the rancid commentators[18] who had twisted the meaning of the word 'elites' to use it against middle-class critics of government policy could hurl it at Aroha or Helen, both informal critics of the policy of mandatory detention. Expressing sympathy for asylum seekers, Aroha said she worried about the children. Aroha's hard life hadn't crushed her generous spirit, and Helen was no different. In her own quiet way, she had things in perspective. Rather than envying people who earned $1500 a week, she felt sorry for people with nothing. The refugees should be allowed into the country, she said. Why not let the people whose lives have been so hard settle here like immigrants always had? But the people already here didn't want to share, she said, surprisingly firm on the subject. 'People want to hold on to everything they have. That's the trouble.'

Because it was my last day, I half-expected a reprieve of some sort but there was none. People still had to be fed. Dishes still had to be washed. The trolleys of dirty dishes were blocking the doorway again, and Helen and I talked as I scraped and stacked plates and she cleaned up on the other side of the kitchen. She said she enjoyed working with me, and I turned to grin at her. 'I know I wasn't any good at the job. I'm really a writer,' I said, hoping it explained everything. I don't know what it says about the relative place of newspapers and books in the world, but my revelation about writing a book reverberated only when I said I usually worked for a newspaper. Helen looked shocked, as if this was something she needed to go off and think about, which she did a moment later, taking out some garbage and staying outside for a smoke. If she was disconcerted, I, for my part, had behaved characteristically, spilling the beans before I started worrying about the consequences, assuring Helen, who looked at me blankly, that she wouldn't be identified.

But I still had work to do. I still had to cart out the rest of the garbage, mop the floors, and put paper mats on the trays, maintaining a semblance of gentility for residents spoon-fed baby food. I had farewelled Helen and was signing the timesheet one last time, putting in overtime with a flourish as I always did, not that I would be paid for it, when Bill, a fresh-faced resident of about 70, a retired railway worker, asked if I was from the office. The first few times I met Bill he talked about his home in the country and what they did there. 'We used to have plenty of that up at Singleton,' he had said in his bluff way when I had given him orange juice that morning. But by the time I spoke with him again, he was in evident distress. He wanted to go home, he said, but they were keeping him locked up. I stayed talking awhile, then looked for someone to ease his mind, but the staff were in a meeting in the dining room. I waved as I went past, and drifted out of their lives, payslip in my hand.

I had been classified as a personal care attendant, rather than a kitchen hand, a slip that provoked me to investigate. The award rate for nurses and domestics in private, for-profit nursing homes was then $481 gross a week, or $12.65 an hour. Vera had paid me $11.72 an hour, ripping off my sub-standard minimum wages by 93 cents an hour, refused to pay overtime, and failed to pay for the training. What a class act. (In 2004, the Labor Party promised to set up a $40 million fund to help underpaid workers recover their wages and entitlements. Labor's workplace relations spokesman, Dr Craig Emerson, said that in 2003 the Howard government had prosecuted only seven such cases throughout Australia, failing to prosecute underpayments below $10,000, though there had been more than 5000 complaints about underpayment in a single year.)[19]

I pocketed $301.55 for an alleged 31 hours (when I worked more than 38), but at least there was no biblical quotation. The message on the bottom of the payslip I picked up the last day I worked for Excelsior was: 'Let us not love in word or speech, but in deed and in truth.' (1 John 3:18). I may have earned $212 for my eighteeen and a half hard hours, getting $14.86 an hour, about 40 cents an hour over the award for the 'Charitable Sector Aged and Disability Care Services Rate', but I wasn't in the market for improving thoughts, especially when I saw the washing I would have to deal with after Bev went home for the day. I felt I'd been tricked somehow. There I was in the laundry with 22 large laundry bags of sheets and undersheets, tablecloths, pillowcases and 'personals' to fold, bag and drag out to the boxroom where Arthur picked them up. Slow at folding sheets, I bundled them up bent out of shape like origami, thinking about the treatment of casual employees by the good Christian people up in the office. I would decline several days' work when one of them phoned at the end of that week, but as I stood there, folding the interminable piles, I felt unreasonably annoyed that I hadn't been offered more shifts. I knew I was never coming back, even if *they* didn't, but I seethed anyway.

I may have spent the best part of a year in and out of the low-wage workforce doing things I'd never done before, from cleaning hotel toilets to laundering loads of institution washing, but I had failed to adapt to the real indignity, being treated as a person of no consequence. I kept waiting to be consulted, about my own schedule, at least. I couldn't get it through my head that I was just another set of hands. My co-workers dealt with it by distancing themselves from the contempt implicit in the management's attitudes.

When I grabbed the last seat at lunchtime, the crew around the picnic table was talking about a long-gone manager. 'There was so-and-so,' Lillian said in her sing-song voice. 'That was another one that was going to walk on water.' Lillian had lost count of the number of managers who had come and gone in her fourteen years at Excelsior. But another date was on her mind. It was her wedding anniversary, which reminded her of her honeymoon decades before. 'We had a caravan up at Terrigal, one of those little old ones,' she said. She had asked a woman she met to the caravan for a cuppa, bursting with pride

THE HOMES

because it was a place of her own. Someone else at the picnic table asked her if she was going out for the anniversary. 'Just to the bowling club,' Lillian said, with the same droll expression on her face. It came to me that she was that rarest of creatures – a person satisfied with her lot in life.

Back in the laundry, I asked Bev, who was about to knock off, to nominate the worst job she had ever done. I told her the worst I'd had was in an egg factory in the bush. But Bev couldn't think of one. 'I've been lucky, I suppose.'

EPILOGUE

THERE WAS A TIME, not so long ago, when Australians prided themselves on giving people a fair go. Now we seem more inclined to blame people for lagging behind. And there are more lagging behind than ever. According to recent figures from the United Nations,[1] about one in eight people in Australia live in poverty, a failure that stands in stark contrast to the successes elsewhere. Out of seventeen highly developed nations, Australia manages to have the third-highest quality of life[2] *and* the third-largest percentage of people living below the poverty line. Despite a prolonged burst of prosperity that has seen the nation withstand worldwide economic trends, the ruthless restructuring that accounts for its new-found efficiency has left almost one in five families jobless.[3] Those who do have work include 2.3 million casual workers who are largely denied 'the perks of permanency – respect, security, predictability, paid holidays and sick days.'[4] More than one in four Australian workers are casuals, pining for 'perks' like job security; one in three part-time workers want more work than they have; two-thirds of young people have no choice but to enter the labour market as casuals; and the most comprehensive Australian study of the changes in the workplace wrought by twenty or so years of the vaunted economic reforms[5] suggests that one-third of the workforce will be casually employed by the end of the current decade.

Confronted with such figures, representatives of business organisations almost invariably demand more of the same, promoting the fiction that workplace reform benefits employees by giving them more choice over the conditions of their employment,[6] a theme continued by the Howard Government. When the election of 2004 gave it effective control of both houses of parliament, the government immediately promised to press on with its program of labour market deregulation.[7] High on the agenda is exempting businesses that employ fewer than twenty people from the unfair dismissal laws, to save small business owners the trouble of following set procedures before firing employees.

Members of the overclass who promote such reforms have only profited from them, to judge from the widening wealth

EPILOGUE

gap.[8] Unabashed, they continue to scold low-wage workers about the need for wage restraint. Unceasing in their efforts to crank up the revolution they started (as if building a new country on the unloved bones of the old), columnists on six-figure salaries rail against regular increases in the minimum wage, now $24,700 a year. Leading commentators claim that attempts to even up the widening inequalities constitute a failed form of 'social engineering' – even, God forbid, 'a nostalgia for pre-80s egalitarianism'.[9] They often point to the United States to bolster the argument that keeping wages low creates jobs, but this argument was less convincing by 2004. On 19 August the *New York Times* reported: 'The labor market adds only a trickle of new jobs each month despite nearly three years of uninterrupted economic growth . . . there are still about a million fewer jobs in the United States than there were at the beginning of 2001.' Whether or not low-wage workers in the United States earn enough to cover the rent on a trailer home, they earn more than the workers in the countries now doing most of the manufacturing.

When I returned to Australia in 1991, after living in the United States for more than a decade, I was dismayed by the signs that Australia was following its lead, with a labour market increasingly divided between an affluent elite and a low-paid service class. In a nation that had been a model of egalitarianism, fairness and equity now barely got a hearing. By 2001, more than one in eight employees were on a low wage,[10] an indicator of working poverty that had risen substantially in the previous decade, in spite of the boom.[11] But its victims were all but invisible. The opinion-makers had succeeded in shifting the focus from failure to success – from those who were struggling to make ends meet to the so-called aspirational voters, who were doing a bit better. I began *Dirt Cheap* in the hope of telling the other side of the story, from the inside out.

In my experience as a low-wage worker, the jobs all had one thing in common: I no sooner took them on than I, like my fellow employees, seemed to be rendered invisible. I was no longer consulted on my schedule, nor burdened with explanations about the nature of the work I was being hired to do. I found the lack of respect for employees most noticeable in the largest company I worked for, which doesn't bode well for the other half-million or so casuals in retail, the fastest growing industry in Australia. And I left the Store only to be hired by a corporation that didn't bother to spell out the terms of my employment – a lapse I took to be typical of its dealings with casual employees.

It was as if I existed only as part of a class of people doing menial work for minimum wages, a particular irony considering how few of the people I met identified themselves as working class. Like everyone else in society, they were encouraged to think of themselves as individuals, with the freedom to sign individual contracts. The one I signed, on starting work with the hotels, was presented to me as if my signature on the piece of paper was a mere formality. I wouldn't say I was pressured to sign,[12] but doing so finalised the process that made me a permanent employee of the hotels. In effect, this workplace agreement gave the company complete call on my time, 24/7, and didn't include penalty rates for working weekends.

Although I began this book convinced that Australia was emulating the United States by creating a class of the working poor, I've since concluded that minimum-wage employees are generally protected against the real ravages of poverty *as long as they work full-time*. This is especially the case if they are the workers most often invoked by the advocates of deregulation, namely the 45 per cent of the low-wage workers from households with a second, higher income. I didn't meet one employee washing dishes or mopping floors who went home at night to a wealthy spouse, but many of the older, married workers I met were managing to pay off mortgages on houses on the city's edge by scrimping and saving elsewhere. My friend from the egg factory owned a share of a business in her home town, and my friend from the Princess Hotel had put a deposit on a flat, after she and her husband, an invalid pensioner, had almost paid off their house. This was a far cry from the situation in the United States, where full-time employees earning five or six dollars an hour don't have recourse to the government benefits available in Australia for the working poor who, for one reason or another, are forced to work part-time.

Life on minimum wages is harsh – perhaps those advocating

freezing the wages of the lowest paid should try it for themselves, limiting their outings to Hungry Jack's once every three months, like my colleagues at the hotel. But it was when I entered the 'zone of intermittent employment', waiting for days on end to hear if I was to get a single shift, that I met employees desperately working two jobs a day just to make ends meet. Of course, there are those who will complacently suggest that poverty ain't what it used to be, when the poor didn't have a pot to piss in, let alone a broken 'entertainment device'.[13] I can only recommend that they spend more time with nursing home attendants doing double shifts, or with teenagers trying to support themselves – or themselves and their tertiary studies – on junior rates of pay.

But entranced as I had been by the prospect of doing so myself, the reality was daunting. I tried but failed to do what millions of Australians do every day, struggling to support themselves and their families on $475 a week – more than half the average rent for a two-bedroom flat in Melbourne or Sydney. I managed to live on my income only because I had no one else to support and no bills outstanding. I paid for my private health insurance, my home insurance, and the costs of keeping my car on the road out of my savings. I put the $1868 for the car on my credit card and tried to forget it, but $1868 is hard to forget when it takes a month to earn.

When I started this project I was presumptuous enough to believe that in trying to describe what I found, I would be keeping faith with my fellow employees. I had no idea if they would agree. Some seemed to have trouble believing that anyone would bother to write – let alone read – a book about their working lives. Though some were suspicious, I was often looked after by fellow employees quick to share their knowledge of the job and ready to protect me from my frequent mistakes. Such experiences helped to replace my illusions with something more profound: a gut-wrenching understanding of what it is to spend your working hours unappreciated, underpaid and unseen.

Endnotes

Prologue
1. Labor Party analysis of tax figures, published in *The Australian* on 12 January 2004.
2. J. Borland, B. Gregory and P. Sheehan (eds), *Work Rich, Work Poor: Inequality and Economic Change in Australia*, Centre for Strategic Economic Studies, Victoria University of Technology, Melbourne, 2001.
3. *Safety Net Review*, AIRC, 2003.
4. Casual jobs accounted for two-thirds of the increase in total employment from 1990 to 2002, according to Ian Watson, John Buchanan, Iain Campbell and Chris Briggs, *Fragmented Futures: New Challenges in Working Life*, Federation Press, Sydney, 2003.
5. 'One out of three Australians aged between 15 and 64 now rely on welfare benefits at some stage during the year, compared with one in four in 1982.' Quoted in *The Australian*, 11 July 2003, from research by Melbourne University economists Yi-Ping Tseng and Roger Wilkins published in *Economic Record*.
6. Sol Encel, *Age Can Work*, quoted in the *Sydney Morning Herald*, 28 February 2004.
7. Tony Abbott, December 2000, when he was employment minister, quoted in Fred Argy, *Where to from Here? Australian Egalitarianism under Threat*, Allen & Unwin, Sydney, 2003.

Chapter 1: The Club
1. The *Sydney Morning Herald* of 1 December 2001 quoted Tony

Abbott as saying: 'People who want jobs are in areas where the people who want workers are not.'
2 Census data from 2001 indicated that nearly one-third of all Sydney households that paid rent spent 30 per cent or more of their gross incomes on housing costs, quoted in the *Sydney Morning Herald*, 12 August 2002.
3 Seventy per cent of US employers drug-test candidates when ready to make them a job offer, according to the American Management Association, quoted in *LA Times*, 15 December 1999.

Chapter 2: The Factory
1 The federal minimum wage was then $11.35 an hour, or about $431 gross a week. It had gone up to $11.80 an hour, or $448 a week, by March 2003, when the Australian Council of Social Service (ACOSS) put in a submission to the national wage case. Based on benchmarks from the Budget Standards Project at the Social Policy Research Centre at the University of New South Wales, ACOSS argued that 'the modest but adequate benchmark for a single person of workforce age living alone and renting privately' was a disposable income of about $445 a week – equivalent to a gross income of $550 a week, about $100 more than the minimum. The ACOSS submission argued that, since the early 1980s, minimum award wages had fallen substantially relative to 'average weekly ordinary time earnings'.
2 Patricia Karvelas, in '$30m. to Bail Out Ailing Job Network', *The Australian*, 11 July 2003, reports that the government has been forced to prop up the privatised job search networks.
3 Elisabeth Wynhausen, 'Workers' Paradise Lost', *The Australian*, 3 March 1999.
4 Between 1982 and 2002 the proportion of Australian employees working 50 or more hours a week increased from 22 to 29 per cent for males and from 17 to 21 per cent for all employees. Over the same period, the proportion of employees working a standard 35- to 40-hour week fell from half to one-third, according to Watson, Buchanan, Campbell and Briggs, 2003.
5 Between 1995 and 2001 the proportion of full-time employees who would prefer to work less rose from 19.5 to 36.7 per cent; for the

16 per cent of the labour force working more than 49 hours a week, the proportion went up from 38.1 to 58.2 per cent. See Humphrey McQueen, 'Labour's Love Lost', *The Australian*, 18–19 January 2003.

Chapter 3: The Office
1. Global Exchange, a human rights group in the United States, revealed that the dollar value of the wages Nike contractors in Indonesia paid their workers dropped from US$2.47 a day in 1997 to US$0.80 a day, with the fall of the rupiah in 1998. See Naomi Klein, *No Logo*, Knopf, New York, 2000.

Chapter 4: The Hotels
1. By 2003, state privacy commissions in Australia were registering significant increases in the number of queries and complaints about 'surveillance/physical privacy' (Privacy NSW *Annual Report 2002/03*). Some Australian states had introduced legislation to protect workers' privacy, but video surveillance in the workplace remained unregulated.
2. Elisabeth Wynhausen, 'Dirty deeds done cheap', *The Australian*, 29–30 November 2003: 'The ferocious competition for cleaning contracts means immigrant cleaners desperate for work get ripped off by subcontractors willing to exploit their own.' The employees know what they're supposed to earn but don't press it because they're illegals, students exceeding their permitted working hours, or welfare recipients who haven't declared the additional income.

Chapter 5: The Store
1. According to Watson, Buchanan, Campbell and Briggs, 2003, 44.8 per cent were casual by 2002.
2. 'I'd estimate that 75 per cent of the top 400 firms use personality tests . . .' Kevin Chandler of the Chandler Macleod Group, quoted in www.smh.com, 8 July 2004.
3. Watson, Buchanan, Campbell and Briggs, 2003, reveal that the remaining full-time jobs are less likely to incorporate once-basic entitlements such as annual leave and sick leave. By 2003, 13 per cent of the full-time jobs – and about two-thirds of the part-time jobs – were casual.

4 *The Age*, 18 June 2002.
5 Common sense suggested the opposite and common sense had research on its side. In *Why We Buy: The Science of Shopping*, Touchstone, New York, 1999, Paco Underhill reports, 'Marketing, advertising, promotion and location can bring shoppers in, but then it's the job of the merchandise, the employees and the store itself to turn them into buyers.'
6 Barbara Pocock, Roslyn Prosser and Ken Bridge, 'Only a Casual: How Casual Work Affects Employees, Households and Communities in Australia', *Labour Studies*, University of Adelaide, July 2004, quote Barney, a 67-year-old security guard: 'You're only one pay-day away from bankruptcy.' (www.arts.adelaide.edu.au/social sciences/people/gls/bpocock.html).
7 Pocock, Prosser and Bridge, 2004, interviewed 55 casuals. 'I see other women come to work all the time leaving their sick kids at home because they had no choice but to work,' said one, a cashier in her forties.
8 'Casual Work and Casualisation: How Does Australia Compare?' A report by Dr Iain Campbell, RMIT, delivered at the 'Work Interrupted: Casual and Insecure Employment' Conference, Melbourne, August 2004. Campbell analysed ABS figures on employee earnings, benefits and trade union membership for August 2003 to estimate that, if owner–managers are excluded, casual employment represents 25.4 per cent of all employees, or about 20.1 per cent of the workforce.
9 Campbell in 'Casual Work and Casualisation' says: 'our version of casual work is unusual . . . In most other OECD countries it is not possible legally to deprive employees of so many standard rights and benefits.' Campbell points out that the one immediate comparison is with the United States, where some 23 per cent of employees don't get paid holidays whether they work part-time or full-time.
10 Underhill in *Why We Buy* says: 'Shoppers want to experience merchandise before buying it.'
11 Campbell, 'Casual Work and Casualisation'.
12 The Household, Income and Labour Dynamics in Australia (HILDA) survey revealed that in 2001 about one-third of part-time

workers would have preferred to work more hours; 71 per cent of them were employed as casuals.
13 *Sydney Morning Herald*, 12 August 2002.
14 Between 1988 and 2001 in Australia, casual employment for workers aged fifteen to 29 grew from 38 to 66 per cent, according to Watson, Buchanan, Campbell and Briggs, 2003. The authors observe that 'for many young adults casual employment is now their only port of entry into paid employment.'
15 Pocock, Prosser and Bridge, 'Only a Casual'.
16 In *The Work/Life Collision*, Federation Press, Sydney, 2003, p. 52, Dr Barbara Pocock observes that the social community of the workplace is all the more significant given the breakdown of community elsewhere.
17 Sixty-four per cent of women, and 72 per cent of men, according to a 2000 survey quoted by Pocock in *The Work/Life Collision*.
18 With employees in the United States initiating more and more overtime cases under the *Fair Labor Standards Act*, the *Wall Street Journal Online*, 13 June 2002, reported that the Coca-Cola Bottling Co. of Los Angeles had settled a suit for US$20 million, and SBC Pacific Bell had settled a suit for US$35 million. Wal-Mart has been sued for overtime by employees and former employees in 28 states. They say they were ordered to clock off after eight hours, then had to continue working without pay.
19 'We have divided the workforce into real workers and not-so-real workers,' said Belinda Probert, then head of the School of Social Sciences at RMIT, quoted in *The Australian*, 1–2 September 2001.
20 Pocock, Prosser and Bridge, 'Only a Casual'.

Chapter 6: The Homes
1 The future of the Lansdowne Caravan Park near Fairfield, Sydney, which housed 500 people, many just one step up from homelessness, provoked a battle between Meriton Properties, which wanted to remove the vans and develop it and the council and community workers trying to retain it. See Adele Horin, *Sydney Morning Herald*, 14–15August 2004.
2 According to *The Care of Older Australians: A Picture of the Residential Aged Care Workforce*, 2004, a report for the Minister for Ageing's

Workforce Committee by Professor Sue Richardson and Professor Bill Martin of the National Institute of Labour Studies, Adelaide, 57 per cent of the aged care workforce is over the age of 45.

3. In the financial year 1999/2000, private operators of aged care facilities received 74 per cent of their income from government funding – while the not-for-profit providers received 66 per cent – but the formula for government funding of nursing homes is based on the number of residents and the level of care they require, not on the number of staff employed. They can employ as many, *or as few*, as they like. In its submission to the Senate Inquiry into Aged Care in 2004, the Liquor, Hospitality and Miscellanous Workers Union (LHMU) contended: 'Aged care workers regularly work unpaid overtime, just to meet their own sense of obligation to the frail and aged Australians that are dependent on their care.'

4. In 'Eight Days a Week', *Sydney Morning Herald*, 27–28 July 2002, Sherrill Nixon noted that of the few countries bucking the world trend of working shorter hours, Australia was the only one 'in which the trend is driven strongly by increases in unpaid overtime right across the workforce.'

5. Patricia Karvelas, 'Centrelink top-heavy', *The Australian*, 12–13 June 2004.

6. This was considerably less than the casual loading Australian Chamber of Commerce and Industry chief executive Peter Hendy claimed was standard. 'Casual employees are getting a penalty loading of 20–30 per cent. That would have to be taken away. There's no free lunch here – it's one or the other,' Hendy commented after Labor said that many casuals would prefer permanent part-time work. *The Australian*, 6 January 2004.

7. Environmental Media Services quotes a US Environmental Protection Agency study which showed that indoor levels of air pollutants may be much higher than outdoor levels – 'and cleaning products . . . are among the culprits.'

8. Watson, Buchanan, Campbell and Briggs, 2003, found that by 2002, 22.5 per cent of employees in health and community services were casuals with no leave entitlement.

9. Richardson and Martin, 2004, surveyed more than 6000 employees in residential aged care and found that only 13 per cent of nurses,

and 19 per cent of all workers, believed they had enough time to properly care for residents.
10   In its campaign preceding the annual minimum wage case before the Australian Industrial Relations Commission in 2004, the ACTU published a research paper suggesting that productivity levels in three award-dependent industries – hospitality, retail, and health and community services – had soared, but wage levels had remained stagnant 'and as a result real unit labour costs have fallen.'
11   Richardson and Martin, 2004.
12   In his *Pricing Review of Residential Aged Care*, a report for the federal government released in 2004, Professor Warren Hogan found that between 52.7 and 80.3 per cent – an across-the-board average of 66 per cent – of total expenses went on wages.
13   According to Craig Thompson, National Secretary of the Health Services Union, 'There are nursing homes where family and friends are performing the role of paid carers because there aren't enough staff to look after residents.'
14   In 2004 the federal government's National Occupational Health and Safety Commission found that about half of all new worker's compensation claims over the previous six years had occurred in four industries, including the health and community services sector.
15   According to a Health Services Union submission to the Senate Inquiry into Aged Care in 2004, 'at one facility in western Sydney a single carer is rostered on to look after 168 residents in three separate buildings connected by external corridors.' The submission cites reasons for the staff shortages, 'the most important being the regulation and scrutiny of aged care providers', further suggesting that 'the international shortage of nurses, low pay rates, poor working conditions and, increasingly, high stress levels' also play a part.
16   Richardson and Martin, 2004, found that 75 per cent of workers in aged care were satisfied with their jobs despite the stress levels and the low pay, apparently because many had gone back to work after a time at home and felt they were doing something useful.
17   In July 2004, in an apparent policy reversal, Immigration Minister Amanda Vanstone said the 9500 holders of Temporary Protection Visas – namely, asylum-seekers released from detention – could

apply for migration visas. Refugee advocates rapidly declared that it was a trick. The government had failed to alter eligibility criteria which meant most TPV-holders would eventually be rejected for permanent residency.
18 Michael Duffy, 'Outraged Elite All Lost at Sea', *Daily Telegraph*, 8 September 2001.
19 *Sydney Morning Herald*, 7–8 August 2004.

Epilogue
1 *Human Development Report*, 2004.
2 Assessed by ranking such indicators as life expectancy, literacy and standard of living, as measured by GDP.
3 Eighteen per cent of families are jobless, according to George Megalogenis in 'The Missing Breadwinner', *The Weekend Australian*, 10–11 July 2004, p. 17, who found that more than 660,000 dependent children are growing up in jobless households.
4 Pocock, Prosser and Bridge, 2004, found that three-quarters of the casual workers interviewed for the study were pining for these perks.
5 Watson, Buchanan, Campbell and Briggs, 2003.
6 'Our conclusion is that the failure to maintain the pace of labour market reform has denied people access to the labour market in the form they want it . . .' said Peter Anderson, Director of Workplace Policy for the Australian Chamber of Commerce and Industry, in 2003, when asked about the alarming evidence presented in Watson, Buchanan, Campbell and Briggs, *Fragmented Futures*, 2003.
7 'The prime minister would say the highest priority would be industrial relations reform,' Senator Robert Hill told the *Adelaide Advertiser*, 'In Control', 11 October 2004.
8 In 'Home and Hosed', *Sydney Morning Herald*, 10–11 July 2004, Andrew Stevenson and Lisa Pryor reported that a study for the *Herald* by NATSEM showed that the wealth of the richest 20 per cent of people in Sydney had risen from an average of $450,000 in 1994 to $863,000 ten years later, while the wealth of the poorest 20 per cent had risen from less than $4,000 to a scant $13,000.
9 To quote Peter Dawkins and Paul Kelly (eds), *Hard Heads, Soft Hearts: A New Reform Agenda for Australia*, Allen & Unwin, Sydney,

2003, who wish to see minimum wage increases replaced by tax credits for low-wage workers – a proposal associated with the five economists, including Dawkins, who first put it forward in 1998.

10   Some 11.3 per cent of males and 14.2 per cent of females, according to Watson, Buchanan, Campbell and Briggs, 2003.

11   Between June 2002 and June 2003, 'Private wealth in Australia jumped 14.7 per cent to an all-time high' on the back of surging house prices which had risen about 20 per cent in 2002, according to a report in the *Sydney Morning Herald*, December 2003, entitled: 'Richer than ever – and feeling so good about it'.

12   Unlike childcare workers I have interviewed since, who reported that ABC Learning Centres, the largest private childcare provider in Australia, put some young childcare workers in a room with three company executives before producing the workplace agreement. Under the terms of that contract, minimum-wage employees earning about $13.30 an hour agreed to pay for their own police checks and first-aid training, and to purchase their own uniforms through the company.

13   The best we can do these days is 'relative poverty' according to right-wing polemicist Peter Saunders, whose issue paper 'Getting the Facts Right About Poverty' Centre for Independent Studies, Sydney, 2002, claims that only 5 per cent of Australians are so poor they are prevented from participating 'in the normal life of the society', thus excluding from his definition of 'relative poverty' large numbers of social security recipients making do on $12,000 a year.